POWER

TALK

**Insights from Asia's
Leading Entrepreneurs**

POWER TALK

Insights from Asia's Leading Entrepreneurs

Karen Lam

World Scientific

NEW JERSEY • LONDON • SINGAPORE • BEIJING • SHANGHAI • HONG KONG • TAIPEI • CHENNAI • TOKYO

Published by

World Scientific Publishing Co. Pte. Ltd.
5 Toh Tuck Link, Singapore 596224
USA office: 27 Warren Street, Suite 401-402, Hackensack, NJ 07601
UK office: 57 Shelton Street, Covent Garden, London WC2H 9HE

Library of Congress Cataloging-in-Publication Data
Names: Lam, Karen, author.
Title: Power talk : insights from Asia's leading entrepreneurs / Karen Lam.
Description: New Jersey : World Scientific, 2018.
Identifiers: LCCN 2018018583| ISBN 9789813235120 (hardback) |
    ISBN 9789813236202 (pbk.)
Subjects: LCSH: Executive ability--Asia. | Chief executive officers--Asia. |
    Success in business--Asia. | Entrepreneurship--Asia. | Business enterprises--Asia.
Classification: LCC HD38.25.A78 L34 2018 | DDC 658.0095--dc23
LC record available at https://lccn.loc.gov/2018018583

British Library Cataloguing-in-Publication Data
A catalogue record for this book is available from the British Library.

For any available supplementary material, please visit
http://www.worldscientific.com/worldscibooks/10.1142/10853#t=suppl

Desk Editor: Sylvia Koh

Typeset by Stallion Press
Email: enquiries@stallionpress.com

About the Author

Karen Lam has been a media and business consultant for over 20 years, helping organisations in the region in the areas of presentations and media communication. In 2012, she took on another role, returning to her first love in television as host and series producer of the business personality series, *Power List Asia*, on Channel NewsAsia.

Karen started off her career as a broadcast journalist with the general news desk of Singapore Broadcasting Corporation (now known as Mediacorp). She covered local stories interviewing politicians, business people and other newsmakers in the local and international scenes. She later went on to anchor the nightly news.

When the opportunity to explore the world of corporate training arose, Karen jumped at it to get perspectives into people development and business operations from a variety of industries and countries. The opportunities she's had to rub shoulders with captains of industry, to walk the factory floors with them and hear from the people who keep the organisations running — both on and off camera, as a journalist and as a consultant — has given her rare insights into the intricacies and vicissitudes of business in Asia.

Acknowledgement

A book that originates from a journey that began years ago can only be a montage of people, circumstances and providence. It is not the work of one.

I owe my deepest gratitude to my former colleague and friend, Debra Soon, who opened the way for me to host the programme. To pick me out after having left the business for close to 20 years is either great prescience or reckless foolhardiness. After six seasons of the show, I'd like to think it's the former.

With the various executive producers I've worked with and who've pushed me for more, I can finally say thank you. Mok Choy Lin, Huang Weixian, Christopher Hale, Ruth Pereira, it's been my pleasure to be challenged by the best. And to the producers who have been my partners in crime, I owe this book to your hard work — Ikhwan Rivai, Pearl Forss, Asha Popatlal, Lolita Lachica, Amelia Loh, Shehzad Hameed Ahmad, Sumithra Prasanna, Kenny Giam and Vaani Balasubramaniam.

For the book to be even completed, I owe my gratitude to Chua Hong Koon who guided me from the start to think about how I could make my work last as long as the Bible. Such was the divine standard set for me and that compelled me to dig deeper each time I was content with enough.

I'm also thankful to my editor, Philly Lim, for being ever so patient with me, particularly during the times when I was running around higgledy-piggledy, not knowing what I'd sent in for reviews and what I'd worked on. And those days were many. Ever the provocateur, she often bore the brunt of my annoyance each time she probed me with what I wanted to sweep aside as irrelevant and uninformed questions but, in calmer moments, saw the validity of the enquiries. Thanks, too, to Sylvia Koh, for picking up the pieces and having such a keen eye for details.

Many trusted friends came along the way to plod through various parts of the books while it was still brewing. I'm indebted to Daniel Khaw, Daniel Ho, Jason Lee, Melinda Yeoh and Jerad Tan.

And to the ones who had to bear with my volatility while I experienced birth pangs and who cheered me on, I can only say you are my champions — my children, Ewan and Emma, and my soul mate for life, Jit Cheng. Your belief in me, even when there wasn't much to go on, kept me going.

Ultimately, I owe it all to the driver behind the wheel, my Creator who called me by name and for whom this book is a sacred work for it comes from hands that have been redeemed, a life that's been saved and a heart that's been transformed by the real Power from on high.

Foreword

To understand the genesis of Karen Lam's book, one needs to understand the connection between her, myself, and Channel NewsAsia. Between 2012 and 2013, as managing director of Channel NewsAsia, I had argued for and got the budget to turn the channel into a 24-hour news channel, up from 18 hours. Beyond transmitting more news, the vision was really to become the number one channel to help viewers around the world "understand Asia".

The mission was to reflect the diversity, multiplicity and complexity of Asia, not presenting one perspective, but a nuanced view informed by being in Asia, understanding the cultural context of Asia, from South to South-east and North-east.

It was a tall order.

We had to take a really hard look at what the channel put out and improve the content significantly. Instead of superficial news content rewritten from other sources, we had to beef up our reporting from the region with our own correspondents. Beyond that, we had to create solid non-news programming that would resonate with viewers. I was on a talent hunt, in a limited pool. I was on a mission.

I invited Karen to be part of that guerilla troupe, and from 2012, she was the face (and brains) for *Power List Asia*.

As a trained television journalist, Karen has been able to sieve opinions and insights from facts; she had a disarming and intelligent presence which no doubt helped to charm the *Power List* interviewees into revealing more about themselves on screen than they would normally have done. And this has to be done in a concise and engaging manner, in conversational prose. Karen has managed to turn this on screen content into a book, writing in an accessible, readable and entertaining style, whilst revealing insights into the personalities she spoke to.

In today's noisy, crowded, information overloaded environment, books are no longer fashionable. On top of that, there is an endless stream of information, from a multiplicity of sources which have to be verified. The sinister side of technology has reared its head, making it easy for deliberate misinformation and fake news to be proliferated. Instead of spending time trying to read about successful entrepreneurs in Asia from the internet, pick up this book instead.

What drives success in Asia? How did the pioneers do what they did, how are they planning their succession? What are their views on life and family?

Karen's interviewees are a veritable who's who of Asia. From South, to South-east and to North-east Asia, entrepreneurs who reflect the diversity of Asia, the different routes and paths to success, but who are bound together by common themes of life, family and values.

This is what *Power Talk* has managed to capture, and in essence, what Channel NewsAsia was meant to do.

I am proud that Karen shared the journey with us and congratulate her for writing a book I would recommend to anyone who wants to understand entrepreneurship in Asia.

Debra Soon
Chief Marketing Officer
and Head of Family (English) & Premier Segments
Mediacorp Pte Ltd, Singapore

Contents

Introduction

Who gets paid to travel around Asia, have exclusive one-on-ones with top entrepreneurs, provoke them with questions you'd not ask in normal settings, get under their skin and uncover motivations and regrets — and be thanked by them after all that?

As the host of Channel News Asia's *Power List Asia*, which ran from 2012 to 2017, with 73 episodes over six seasons, 26,000 manhours of pre- and post-production and 130,000 airmiles, I've been bestowed a treasury of stories and lessons from Asia's foremost businessmen and women. It's been a prolonged course by the masters, themselves, of business administration.

Each half-hour episode of the show focusses on one business mogul who's shaped the business landscape of his country, the region and even the world. I've scoured 12 countries in Asia — from the usual suspects like Singapore, China, India, Hong Kong and Indonesia to those from the more obscure territories of Mongolia and Nepal — to dig up stories of inventiveness, entrepreneurship and survival. While the tycoons are synonymous with the business empires they've built, my interest is often piqued by the substance that makes them extraordinary and even the foibles that make them human.

Invariably, the subject of entrepreneurship runs throughout the programme and the focus is on personalities, but I've always found myself necessarily falling short of casting more specific themes that the different magnates bring from their unique journeys — lessons they can collectively expound on. This is a sad consequence of meeting the programming schedule that compels us to push out one personality after another and the very real fact that bringing the specific tycoons together in one season, is virtually impossible.

So, this book is an opportunity to "gather" my guests to highlight personal lessons on handling crises, moving up the value chain by growing brands, taking on western businesses — through competition or acquisitions, the collective experience of the next generation business of technology startups, the wisdom and grit of first generation pioneers who built their empires after World War II, the head honchos who've made leadership communication their hallmarks, succession planning and the positive trend of philanthropy.

While many of the initial technologies and expertise have come from the west, successful Asian businesses have been agile enough to adapt them to their own environments. They've adroitly navigated their way through volatile political vicissitudes and cultural norms while being sensitive to conventions — an instinctive and relational dance that moves forwards and backwards, in time with the different movements and tempos of the different political and economic milieux.

Through the eyes of these foremost business leaders, you'll see how the local landscapes play out to the misfortune of most, but to the triumph of the few. Great heights of success are achieved, sometimes through fortitude, other times through fortuity. Humble beginnings, growth, controversies, challenges, expansion, succession — all the ingredients for a great movie. Who needs fiction when you have real faces and facts that can inspire?

The Asian business landscape has been the focus of the world's attention in the last three decades as developed markets in the west start looking to emerging markets for growth. The meteoric rise of China, the increasing clout of the Asian Tigers of Singapore, Taiwan, South Korea and Hong Kong, the burgeoning growth of Southeast Asia, and of course the irrepressible ascendancy of India have all converged to form the grand moniker *The Asian Century*.

Through these pages, you'll go beyond the broad swaths and platitudes of business Asia to the motivations, instincts and, yes, even the missteps of the people who contribute in significant ways to make this the most vibrant region in the world today.

Part I

THE PIONEERS

Entrepreneurs today have different sets of challenges from those experienced by their predecessors who began their journey about the time of the Second World War. The struggle for the pioneers centred on limited resources and a lack of skilled labour in politically tumultuous times. Today, with advanced technology, access to education and funds, and abundant opportunities, the challenge is not about starting a venture but sustaining it in the midst of global competition and constant innovation.

There's something about the pioneering spirit that never fails to draw us in. Perhaps pioneers from the Silent Generation represent a slice of the past that we no longer have access to and we can only reminisce about, as we do over faded photos of yesteryear. Or, amid the get-rich-quick Ponzi schemes and bubbles that envelope empty promises, we harbour a yearning for times when gall, grit, and gumption laid the foundation of the storied business empires of today.

When we do manage to capture in the flesh, a trailblazer who triumphed over personal adversity, political uncertainty and economic downturns, and who lived through historical events that are part of the pages of our schools' history syllabus, we settle ourselves down with a hot cup of *pu-erh*, ready for a good yarn.

But these occasions are few and far between. Persuading living legends to come on the show is a challenge. Firstly, many of them don't need the publicity. They sit atop empires that already touch the lives of millions. Secondly, in Asia, particularly among the Chinese diaspora, playing down oneself is a virtue. More importantly, their privacy is paramount. Better to lay low than have dirt dug up and tall poppies cut down.

Those who have granted me their time do it for two reasons — a genuine enjoyment of telling their stories to a wider audience and a hope that inspiration will follow for those who resonate with their values. In this season of their lives when there's nothing more to prove and nothing more to lose, it's a response to a higher calling to touch hearts.

Many of the stories that follow are about the visionaries who marched to the beat of their own drums. I've made it a point to bring out the less glamorous aspects of failures, disappointments, and controversies. For aren't these but the flip side of the same coin of success?

I hope you'll be as inspired as I was when I had the privilege to step into their worlds. The road to success, I'd like to believe, is still paved with the same virtues of courage, insights, industry, and yes, a touch of providence.

Chapter 1

The Master Networker

Mochtar Riady
Lippo Group, Indonesia

The study of Mochtar Riady's life is a review of the modern history of both Indonesia and China, in particular the momentous periods that shook the foundations of these two countries and changed them fundamentally.

It's hard to imagine that a man so small in stature and so placid in appearance had lived dangerously through civil wars in Indonesia and China, been exiled for his anti-colonial activities, trudged through the political–business quagmire of the Suharto period, and sunk to the depths in the Asian Financial Crisis, only to emerge with an empire bigger than he had ever dreamed of.

Clad in the signature Indonesian formal wear of the long-sleeved *batik* shirt, Pak Mochtar, as he's known in his home country, embodied a calm befitting a man who's been there, done that, and has nothing else to prove. He wore a perpetual smile that hid a mind that was constantly thinking of the next bit of action. At 86, when I met with him at his office, this octogenarian clocked into work every weekday and Saturday. He was lucid and sharp and would wrestle down any suggestion that he disagreed with, not with brash defensiveness but challenging questions (asked with that smile still on his face) that made me do a double take and wonder if I had my facts right. Nothing escaped him.

Born in 1929, Mochtar Riady, christened Li Wenzheng, is the son of a *batik* trader who moved to Indonesia from Fujian, China. Riady was taken to his father's birthplace at five months old when word of his grandfather's illness reached the family. And there the family stayed for six years.

Tossed about by unrest in Fujian during the Warlord Era, the anti-Dutch protests in Indonesia, and the civil war between the Nationalists and Communists in Nanjing, young Riady shuttled between China and Indonesia in his early years.

Quite the firebrand as a student in Indonesia, Riady opposed the colonialists as president of the East Java Overseas Chinese Students Association. He supported Indonesian guerrillas and participated in anti-Dutch demonstrations.

It was then that his world view was shaped by his socialist mentors.

> I became more sympathetic towards socialism.

"One of my *gurus*, he was an extreme leftist, and he taught me what imperialism and capitalism were about. So, since then, I became more sympathetic towards socialism."

When I pointed out the irony of a socialist becoming a successful capitalist, he chuckled knowingly and said, "That is the story," one that was uncovered in the course of the interview.

Riady had to flee Indonesia for Nanjing during a crackdown on student demonstrators. It was only when the Dutch finally relinquished control of Indonesia, just before the end of 1949, that Riady returned home.

Looking back, Riady acknowledged the value of his war-torn past: "Maybe this is the reason why I am very tough and I can withstand difficult situations," he mused.

The banker extraordinaire

Riady's office, where the interview took place, was not outlandish in its set-up in any way but regally functional. Much like the occupant himself — nothing in his appearance to draw attention to himself but certainly, a giant of a personality.

Riady's Lippo Group is one of Indonesia's largest conglomerates with interests in property, health care, education, retail, hospitality, and banking throughout Southeast Asia, Hong Kong, China, and the US. Revenue of the Group amounted to US$7.5 billion in 2017, and the man himself worth about US$3 billion.[1]

His secretary was nowhere to be seen. The cameras were allowed to be set up, while he worked quietly at his desk. The shifting of the furniture and the instructions among the crew didn't seem to disturb the man as he focused on the day's work.

The reality of the power that he quietly wields became evident when his deputies gathered in his office with bowed respect, akin to reverence even, as each took turns to speak to the patriarch in measured tones. His PR man only spoke to him when needed. But one suspects it's respect, rather than fear, that inspires such care among staff when dealing with Pak Mochtar.

After all, way before most of us were even conceived, ambition was already scorching through his veins. A worthy one but certainly, as his life unfolded, too small for this giant of a magnate.

> 'How can you be a banker? You don't have money.'

Young Riady's drive to succeed was triggered at the age of 10, when he spotted a majestic colonial building that housed a Dutch bank. He was intrigued by the well-dressed employees who stepped into the building. He was to learn later from his school principal how a bank operated and profited.

With that, young Riady declared to his father one day that he would work in a bank when he grew up. Little did he know that he would *own* a few in his lifetime.

But pragmatism was the order of the day for a family that was barely making ends meet. "My father was against me being a banker," Riady revealed. "He said, 'How can you be a banker? You don't have money.'"

Riady went on to relate the conversation between him and his father.

"And then I said, 'The commodity of the bank is not money. It's trust.' He said, 'You don't have the trust. You are poor. You are not a rich man. How can people trust you?' And then I told him, 'I can find someone who is and I can persuade him to be my partner. And then we can run the business.'"

Such was the prophetic vision of a young boy who turned what seemed to be childhood naiveté into reality. Indeed, over time, Riady honed his skill as a master networker, making the right connections at the right time.

Young Riady tried his hand at several jobs as he settled into life in newly-independent Indonesia. One of his early achievements was growing his in-laws' shop into the largest department store in their town in East Java. But restlessness continued to brew in this ambitious young man.

So, he set off for the bright city lights of Jakarta and took up the bicycle trade, a business that Fujianese migrants gravitated towards. Along the way he dabbled in trading textiles and electrical goods before venturing into shipping. His dream, however, of becoming a banker lingered.

Opportunity finally came knocking in 1959 when Riady got wind of a local bank looking for some capital. True to his talent as a networker, Riady gathered a group of investors and pooled together US$200,000 to purchase a 66% stake in Bank Kemakmuran. With ownership came the titles of chairman and general manager.

His dream had finally come true. But it soon became a nightmare when he realised he was in over his head. Day one and he was presented with a balance sheet which he could make no sense of. He had to pick up basic accounting and pick it up fast. And that he did. After a year, he not only knew the workings of the bank but, incredibly, turned the ailing bank around.

But Riady's tenure in the bank was short lived after he discovered unscrupulous practices among the shareholders. He left after vain attempts to set things right.

From the 1949 to 1966, Sukarno ruled Indonesia with an iron fist. He was more intent on pursuing political ends than developing the economy. He cut off links with the West and, by default, the rest of the world, preventing much-needed foreign funds from flowing into the country. Each time the government's coffers ran low, money would be printed. This led to a period of hyperinflation. In 1966, inflation was riding at 635% and interest rates at 24%.

In the meantime, having left Bank Kemakmuran, Riady had his feelers out for other opportunities. He didn't have long to wait. Bank Buana had run into some trouble because of poor management. To take over the small outfit, Riady would have to corral a group of investors to come on board with him. Once again, his wide network came in handy.

Riady turned to his mentor, who was the secretary of the Indonesian Overseas Chinese General Association, a position that made the latter very well connected with the Chinese business community. He introduced one of the city's leading textile businessman to Riady who then set about working on the relationship.

"I played tennis with him every day, and I tried to give him an understanding of the banking business," Riady recalled. Soon, he managed to win the confidence of the influential businessman and included him in a consortium of companies to acquire Bank Buana in 1965. With that, Riady began the work to turn around the ailing bank.

In the tight credit environment at the time, Riady decided to boost Bank Buana's capital by halving the interest rate to 12%, with a condition — borrowers would have to provide collateral to secure the loans (most loans were unsecured then). The risk, if the bold move fell through, was a squeeze on the bank's already tight liquidity. However, as history would have it, it was a gamble that paid off. Bank Buana saw not only the number of non-performing loans slashed as debtors took the proffered olive branch to settle their debts, but other businesses were also drawn to the cheaper money. The collateral they promised boosted the bank's capital and Riady succeeded in rehabilitating yet another troubled bank.

As the banking industry developed in Indonesia, so did the number of banks. In 1968, there were over 130 banks in the country.[3] With a lack of a rigorous regulatory environment, capital, and expertise, coupled with hyperinflation and speculative borrowing, the writing was on the wall — the banking system was headed towards a collapse.

With the reputation and network he had built for himself, Riady persuaded the government to initiate a consolidation of the industry. The fact that he owned four banks by then added weight to his argument. With the central bank's nod, he undertook the first merger of three banks in 1971. Bank Panin was founded.

But the road to success is never smoothly paved. As the bank grew, disputes arose between Riady and the other owners, one of whom was his brother-in-law. In his autobiography, he bemoaned the "shortsightedness"[4] of the shareholders who stood in the way of his vision of making Bank Panin the second clearing house apart from the central bank. Taking up that role, Riady believed, would cement the bank's long-term prospects and make it integral to the banking system in the country.

While the dispute wore on, an offer to run a small bank owned by a very influential businessman came along. Riady took the opportunity to step away from Bank Panin. But not before he left it with assets 12 times more than what it had when it first started.[5]

The crony benefactor

In 1975 when Riady took over Bank Central Asia, or BCA, it had only one office with 27 employees, with assets of no more than US$3 million. But it wasn't the size of the bank that mattered to Riady but who owned it and what could be done through the owner's connections.

Liem Sioe Liong, also known as Sudono Salim, was one of President Suharto's right-hand men. The position came with many lucrative concessions and monopolies that were given to the companies he founded under the Salim Group.

One of these was the licence to import cloves, an important ingredient used in the making of *kretek,* a locally produced cigarette. Unlike Sukarno, Suharto was intent on developing the economy when he took over and one of the pillars of his New Order was the development of indigenous industries — *kretek* being one of them. This Indonesian product would become one of the main drivers of the economy.

Riady recognised that the hand that controlled the import of cloves was a mighty one indeed. That hand belonged to Salim.

"He knew every tobacco factory in Indonesia," said Riady, of his former boss. "So, through him I persuaded all the tobacco factories to be our customers. Then we asked them to introduce their upstream and downstream suppliers, and their retailers. So, all of them became BCA customers." This was low-hanging fruit that Riady spotted from the outset — the expansion of the bank through Salim's wide network.

Salim knew a good man when he saw one. To retain Riady, the owner offered him 17.5% of BCA's equity to keep up the good work. One wonders if Salim would have been so generous if he had foreseen how big the bank would grow under Riady's watch. By the time Riady left the bank, 15 years later, BCA had become Indonesia's largest private bank.

Shortly after he joined BCA, Riady put on another hat and set up a trading company under Lippo Holding, the entity he would later build his empire upon. The name was a combination of the Chinese words *li,* or power, and *pao,* treasure.

Riady was kept busy growing BCA while overseeing the Lippo Group which was managed by his sons. In 1981 Riady was offered a 49% stake in a relatively small lender, Bank Perniagaan Indonesia. It was later merged with another small bank which he owned to form Lippo Bank in 1989. By then, Riady had decided that it was time to focus on his own business and left BCA.

But there was also a push from within that led to his departure.

> Mr Liem's relationship with our past President was too close. I had to separate myself from him.

While Suharto's presidency was marked by significant progress in the economy and international relations, it was also marred by widespread corruption and repressive military crackdowns. It was the Suharto family and their friends who were major recipients of kickbacks and government contracts. One observer had suggested that 80% of government projects were awarded to the Suharto clan and friends.[6] Towards the tail end of the three decades of the president's rule, public opinion against these practices, that used to be quietly tolerated, became increasingly vociferous.

BCA was not only under the control of Salim but also two of Suharto's children who held 30% of the bank's shares.[7] Sensing trouble on the horizon, Riady decided to take his leave from BCA in 1990. His reason for leaving was almost philosophical. "I always believe business and politics have to be separate. We have to be respectful of the politicians, but I don't think that business has to work together with politics."

Later, he accedes, "I think Mr Liem's relationship with our past President was too close," referring to Salim by his Chinese name. "I had to separate myself from him." It was an amicable separation between the two men who had great respect for each other, with a cash-free exchange of shares between BCA and Lippo Bank. In all, it was this prescient move that would save Riady's fortunes during the Asian Financial Crisis of 1997 and the fall of Suharto.

The rise and fall of Lippo Bank

The Lippo Group grew over the years and by 1993, it was the third largest company in the country[8] with other verticals such as finance, property, manufacturing, health care, retail, and cinemas coming into the fold. It set up a second base in Hong Kong to look into its growing business in China. Its main activity there is investment holding with interests in property, food, hospitality, mining and financial services.

At the same time, Lippo Bank was making substantial progress, becoming one of the biggest banks in Indonesia and the first to be listed successfully. If anything, the bank was Riady's crowning achievement. Among all the banks he part-owned and revived, this was the one he had the largest stake in. It bore the name that was synonymous with the Riadys. It was also the one his eldest son, James, led as CEO. This being James' first leadership role, Riady had both professional and personal interests in the development of the bank. It was the culmination of his childhood dream.

The catalyst for Lippo Bank's growth was the government's deregulation policy in 1988 which lifted restrictions on the number of bank branches. Lippo Bank extended its reach and established 106 branches throughout the archipelago in 12 months.[9] It took advantage of the huge population of the unbanked and growing middle class and focused its efforts on retail banking and financing specific industries. A year later it became the second largest private bank, after BCA, with deposits of more than US$1 billion.[10]

But the journey ahead for Lippo Bank was a bumpy one. In 1995, it experienced a bank run that depleted its reserves and required a bail out by five other banks.[11] But even that was nothing compared to the shattering impact of the 1997 Asian Financial Crisis that ripped through the economic fabric of Indonesia, causing the rupiah to plunge more than 80% against the US dollar.[12] Interest rates shot through the roof, hyperinflation prevailed and GDP contracted.

More than anything, the crisis threw the spotlight on the cracks in the entire banking system. Shortcomings that had long been allowed to exist in the regulatory framework and weak corporate governance became starkly evident.

In 1998, Suharto was forced to step down and a bank run ensued on BCA, the bank closely associated with him and his cronies. US$1.2 billion was withdrawn and all who were associated with the Salim and Suharto families were fearing for their lives as protests spilled onto the streets.[13] Chinese businesses, including the Riadys', became easy targets as the population grew increasingly disillusioned by the collapse of the economy. Lippo's flagship mall in Lippo Village was looted and set on fire.

Salim himself fled to Singapore and there he remained until his death in 2012.

The banking system collapsed and the International Monetary Fund (IMF) stepped in. About US$37 billion had to be spent to bail out and re-capitalise banks[14] while a clean-up of the entire banking system took place.

Despite the fact that Lippo Bank was not as exposed to foreign exchange trading as other banks, it still had to write off US$75 million in bad loans.[15] Riady shored up the capital of the bank by pumping in US$225 million after he sold 70% of the Group's life insurance business. But it wasn't enough.

In 1999, Lippo Bank received a cash injection of US$700 million from the government in exchange for a 52% share of the bank. Riady, however, remained commissioner of the bank. The management of Lippo Bank worked hard to fulfil the IMF's conditions by streamlining operations and implementing international best practices, but it remained dogged by controversy.[16]

In 2004, Swiss-Asia Global bought the government's controlling stake in Lippo Bank only to sell it a year later to Malaysia's sovereign wealth fund, Khazanah. In 2005, Riady resigned as commissioner of the bank and, soon after, Lippo Bank ceased to exist as it was renamed CIMB Niaga.

The loss of Lippo Bank resulted in the Group refocusing its efforts on other areas such as property, internet services, and retail. But Riady would not give up the ghost.

In 2010, he re-entered the banking industry in Indonesia when he paid US$6.7 million for a 60% acquisition of Bank Nobu, a small bank with US$600 million in assets and ranked 30th among the commercial banks in the country — a pale comparison to the ones he used to run.

When I raised the point that banking plays a very small role in the Group today, Riady, unfazed, threw a cryptic question back at me.

"Do you think so?" he asked.

The facts speak for themselves but I wondered if I had struck a raw nerve. When I pursued, and

I don't like my sons and my grandchildren to have such an unstable life.

11

asked if he had any regrets on how small the bank's contribution was to the Group, he responded emphatically, "No! No!"

The banking business, Riady rationalised, is not for the faint of heart. In his 50 years as a banker, Riady observed a seven-year cycle before some form of crisis would hit.

"I don't like my sons and my grandchildren to have such an unstable life," he said. This was also the sentiment echoed in the short chapter on the Asian Financial Crisis in Riady's autobiography. The sketchy details in the book belie the tumult those few years wrecked on Lippo Bank, resulting in its sale to the Malaysians.

When I suggested that he was made of much sterner stuff than his children whom he would want to spare the volatility of the banking industry, Riady smiled and conceded graciously, "I don't think my children have such patience to do this."

The socialist returns

Today, the Lippo Group is firmly in the hands of Riady's two sons — James, who runs the business in Indonesia, and Stephen, who operates out of Hong Kong and Singapore to look into interests there and in China and the US. The third generation has started on the journey in the family business and Riady is a contented man.

He expressed confidence in his sons' abilities, having exposed them to the business for more than 20 years while he was at the helm.

"I have a strong belief in my sons," he said. "They are capable."

He is convinced they will do a better job than he.

This frees him to dedicate his time to his current passion — healthcare. Aptly, his office is housed in the eponymous Mochtar Riady Institute for Nanotechnology, a cancer research lab in Lippo Karawaci, the Group's self-contained township about 30 kilometres from Jakarta. His home is a stone's throw away from the office.

Under the Group's healthcare arm, Siloam is a network of 20 hospitals spread across Indonesia. His pet project when we spoke was the launch of an e-medical centre to see to the healthcare needs of second-tier cities. The focus was to close the gap in services between centres such as Jakarta and Surabaya and the smaller towns. With the e-medical centre, patient information from the remote towns can be sent electronically to specialists in Jakarta for their diagnosis.

It's a return to his socialist roots, a call to serve.

"At this moment, I am not thinking about money," Riady said. Rather, it is about his *noblesse oblige*. He holds up prominent philanthropist, the late Tan Kah Kee, who established schools in China and Southeast Asia as his role model.

To that end, the Group has set up an education foundation based on Christian values with schools offering national and international curricula, from kindergarten to tertiary education.

> At this moment, I am not thinking about money.

"My father always advised me — if the family is going to be strong, you have to have good education for the children. If the company is going to be strong, you have to have good people. And for the country or the nation to be a giant, it depends on education," Riady said.

Riady embraced Christianity late in life, at 61. Two decades later and he is still brimming with enthusiasm. The first thing on his mind in the mornings, he said expansively and without missing a beat, was "to glorify God's name."

But can you really be a successful businessperson in Indonesia without compromising your faith? "Christianity tells us you have to work hard and then make as much money as possible. And through this, contribute to the country." The socialist and capitalist do meet, after all, on the path of Christianity.

The Riady family did not reach the heights it has without controversy. The incident that's most often raised to cast aspersions on the family's moral compass is the record US$8.6 million fine that was imposed on Riady's eldest son, James, by the US government. He was found guilty of contributing up to US$700,000 to the Democratic presidential and congressional fundraising campaigns as early as 1988 right up to the President Bill Clinton's first campaign.[17] In their defence, the Riadys said they had not known that overseas funding of political campaigns was illegal.

Speculation had been rife on the Riadys' motivation behind pursuing the Clintons. Observers have suggested they had set themselves up as the unofficial link between the Indonesian and US governments.[18] What is clear, though, is the relationship between the two families began in the 1980s innocently enough when Lippo acquired a bank in Little Rock, Arkansas. Bill Clinton was the governor of the state at that time and the friendship continued through to his presidency.

Riady was reluctant to talk about the Clintons when I brought up the subject. He would only say they hadn't had the opportunity to meet because "I think [Clinton] is a very busy man."

***

As the interview drew to a close and he saw me out of his office, we stopped by a family portrait in the waiting area. It's a wide landscaped photograph of the Riady clan consisting of about 80 people, 4 generations, all dressed in coordinated shades of red, pink, white, and black. You can imagine what a logistical task it must've been to gather this family from all over the world for this occasion. But it obviously was very important to the patriarch as he's given the portrait pride of place in his office — a display to all who enter of what is most important to the man they have come to meet.

Smack in the middle of this illustrious tribe are the patriarch and his wife, the lady who has stood by him through thick and thin. She is also prominently featured in a painted portrait that he has placed right across from the door to his office.

It is telling that Li Limei's eyes follow all who walk in and out of her husband's office. She is the one who has the tycoon's ear on important matters.

Riady related an incident early in his banking career with Bank Buana, when a customer presented him with five sizeable gold bars as a gift. Not having seen ingots before, Riady was thrilled to have them in hand. He brought them home to show them to his wife.

But instead of sharing his delight, she immediately interrogated him. "My wife asked me 'Where does it come from?'" Riady related. "I said it was from one of the customers. She said 'Don't take it. If you receive this gift, that means, you are going to be bound to him and you are going to be a slave to him. So, it's better that you give them back to the owner.' And she insisted, right away, that I had to return it."

Wise words, I suggested, from his better half? He agreed.

For all his successes and challenges, the bouquets and brickbats thrown at him and his family through the years, here is a man who has succeeded from his ability to see opportunities and connect the dots. That he is a master networker is beyond doubt. But through a combination of hard work, smarts, and agility in manoeuvring through crises and peace times, Riady remains today a giant in the Indonesian business landscape.

Here is one who has stood the test of time and who can now, having seen and tasted the best that the world has to offer, return to his socialist roots. He dedicates his time to services to the community and finds his greatest affections in hearth and home.

On his most worthy achievement, this legendary business mogul smiled and acknowledged his family. "I'm very satisfied and very proud," he said. "This is my greatest satisfaction."

Notes

1   "Mochtar Riady & family", Forbes, 5 December 2017, <https://www.forbes.com/profile/mochtar-riady/>

2   "History of Bank Indonesia: Monetary Period 1959–1966", Special Unit of Bank Indonesia Museum, accessed 10 July 2017, <http://www.bi.go.id/en/tentang-bi/museum/sejarah-bi/bi/Documents/bab292dd8e834926a7d7be04e9dfe6c7MicrosoftWordHistoryofMonetaryPeriod19591966.pdf>

3   Yuri Sato, "Banking Restructuring and Reform in Indonesia", The Developing Economies XLIII-1, March 2005, p. 97.

4   Mochtar Riady, Mochtar Riady: My Life Story, John Wiley & Sons, Singapore, p. 61.

5   Rosabeth Moss Kanter, "Using Networking for Competitive Advantage: The Lippo Group of Indonesia and Hong Kong", Strategy + Business, 1 July 1996, <https://www.strategy-business.com/article/17609?gko=17096>

6   Jeffrey A. Winters, Oligarchy, Cambridge University Press, 18 April 2011, p. 170.

7   Mari Pangetsu & Manggi Habir, "The Boom, Bust and Restructuring of Indonesian Banks", April 2002, IMF Working Paper, accessed 10 July 2016, <https://www.imf.org/external/pubs/ft/wp/2002/wp0266.pdf>

8   Natasha Hamilton Hart, Asian States, Asian Bankers: Central Banking in Southeast Asia, NUS Press, 2003, p. 60.

9   Mochtar Riady, Mochtar Riady: My Life Story, Wiley & Sons, Singapore, 2017, p. 153.

10 Rosabeth Moss Kantor, "Using Networking for Competitive Advantage: The Lippo Group of Indonesia and Hong Kong", 1 July 1996, Strategy + Business, Third Quarter 1996/Issue 4.

11 In his autobiography, Mochtar Riady: My Life Story, Riady explained how a minor misdemeanour committed by one of his finance managers sparked off a series of rumours that resulted in a bank run.

    Massive withdrawals went on for a month, depleting the bank's reserves, and this, even after Riady had clarified the situation with the central bank and sought their intervention.

None was forthcoming until Riady threatened to shut the bank. The result of that would have shaken the banking system in Indonesia.

With that, the regulators intervened quietly. Five banks approached Riady with credit lines, including BCA, under the behest of the central bank. The latter needed to be the invisible hand in order not to be perceived as playing favourites as other banks would've cried foul over this bail out. According to Anthoni Salim, the scion of the Salim empire which oversees BCA, about US$800 million was extended to Lippo Bank, all of which was repaid.

12 Anwar Nasution, "The Meltdown of the Indonesian Economy in 1997–1998: Causes and Responses" 30 June 1998, accessed 10 July 2017, <https://www.ids.ac.uk/ids/global/Conf/pdfs/nasut.pdf>

13 Yenni Kwok, "Suharto's Kiss of Death: Seen as crony bank, BCA tries to stem a run" 30 November 2000, Asiaweek.com, accessed 10 July 2017, <http://edition.cnn.com/ASIANOW/asiaweek/98/0612/biz3.html>

14 Mari Pangetsu & Manggi Habir, p. 25.

15 Yasuyuki Matsumoto, *Financial Fragility and Instability in Indonesia*, Routledge, 24 January 2007.

16 This included suspicions that the bank had tried to doctor the books in order to push for a rights issue that would give the family a controlling stake in the bank again. That attempt, however, was thwarted by the government.

17 Sharon LaFraniere, John Pomfret and Lena H. Sun, "The Riadys Persistent Pursuit of Influence" Washington Post, 27 May 1997.

18 LaFraniere, *et al.*

Chapter 2

The Dowager of Chinese Luxury

Balbina Wong
Lane Crawford Joyce Group, Hong Kong

I ronically, the dowager of Chinese luxury is neither a Chinese national nor was she groomed in the lap of luxury. It was through sheer determination, vision, and fortuity that Balbina Wong broke through into a world unlike the one she entered at birth.

Wong founded ImagineX, the premium retail distribution subsidiary of the Hong Kong-based Lane Crawford Joyce Group, in 1992. At the same time, she was also the president and CEO of ImagineX's sister company, Walton Brown. In 1997, she assumed overall management of the Group which is the private enterprise of tycoon Peter Woo, owner of property giant Wheelock and Company.

As the trusted executive of the Woo family business, Wong charted a remarkable course, making Hong Kong the luxury shopping destination of the East and later bedazzling China with brands they just couldn't get enough of.

In 2016, after more than 30 years with the Group, and at 73, she announced her "semi-retirement," working six months in a year. Her biggest relief is not having to pore over the numbers from the 500

points of sale across 50 cities in Greater China and Southeast Asia —
something she was known to do every evening when sales closed for
the day. She still oversees the luxury brands that she's come to be
associated with in Greater China, such as Salvatore Ferragamo, as well
as many others that she's brought in from the West. Her spacious office
has been kept for her — with her secretaries still at her beck and call.

Wong exudes a *joie de vivre* that oozes through
her pores. The very fact that she is a Singapore-born

They call me
Dragon Lady!

Swiss national based out of Hong Kong and married
to an American befuddles the mind and piques
curiousity. She struts around bejewelled and gaited
with a sense of purpose. Her energy puts many of
her younger charges to shame. Speaking to her when she was touching
70 in 2013, she described her younger self with befitting metaphors
that are, like her, larger than life.

"I was like wind and fire in those days. I will never forget when
I used to go to the Frankfurt Fair with the whole buying team, four
or five of them. By the time the fair closed, they were huffing and
puffing. And I was still going on. It was hard for them to keep up
20 years ago," she recalled before conceding. "But today, I will take
my time. I will be at their pace."

Wong's stature in the company is understandably formidable. The
sound of her footsteps can set her employees at attention.

"They call me Dragon Lady!" revealed Wong of her staff. "If I have
to walk through the office now where we have 200–300 people, the
moment they hear my steps, it's all attention. I don't even have to say
a word," she laughed, without a trace of hubris.

All that deference is not for nothing. The reputation Wong has
built for herself over her 30 years charting new courses in Asia and
forming strong alliances in the fashion world has much to do with it.
She has a laser-like vision that comes from an uncanny instinct to zero
in on what consumers want. She is astute and measured in her approach
to new ventures, yet entirely generous and gregarious with people.

From fabric salesgirl to fashion doyenne

Wong's story began in Singapore at the start of the Japanese Occupation.
Her father was an architect who fell ill after the war and remained that
way for a long time. Her mother helped to make ends meet as a caterer.

But with seven children, it was struggle to put food on the table. Wong was the sixth child in the family and at 13, she dropped out of school and became the first of her siblings to start working.

"I was not good at school. We had no money. My mom had seven children," Wong recalled. "So, the sooner I got to work, the better."

There began a two-year stint as a fabric salesgirl. Needless to say, labour laws were virtually non-existent then as the 13-year-old worked 10-hour days, with one day off in a month for two years. All for the princely salary of S$60, some of which went to her mother to support the family.

"I think it's determination. I've always felt I had to do it. I could do it," Wong said of what drove the girl that was barely in her teens to take on such gruel. "My will was very strong to make it happen."

There were times when there was not enough money at home and hunger drove her to steal food from her neighbours. The privation stirred something within young Wong.

"I was determined to succeed and get further," she said.

> Everything was like a step. Nothing like a jump.

And she did. Her next job was as a beauty consultant for the American cosmetics giant at the time, Max Factor, before she joined another beauty brand, Lancome, as a treatment operator doing facials for clients.

Black-and-white snapshots of Wong in her younger days capture a classic Chinese beauty with an hourglass figure wrapped in a cheongsam. Little wonder then, at 19, she caught the eye of a much older Englishman. Len Thorne was a radio personality with Radio Malaya, based out of Singapore. He swept Wong off her feet and off to Hong Kong where they relocated as husband and wife.

The marriage didn't last long but Hong Kong was the land of opportunity that set Wong on her pioneering path. Shortly after landing in the then-English colony, she secured herself a job at Elizabeth Arden as a senior consultant.

There began Wong's ascent through the ranks with other beauty brands before returning to Elizabeth Arden as general manager when she was in her 40s. This new position which came under the Lane Crawford Joyce Group led her along the same path as owner and Hong Kong tycoon Peter Woo, who spotted Wong's rare acumen and handed her the reins of his retail group. She remains one of his trusted lieutenants today.

Wong was mindful to point out that her rise to the top was not a whirlwind overnight phenomenon. As with most things in her life, it was a dogged process. "Everything was like a step. Nothing like a jump," she pointed out.

Of the many luxury brands that Wong brought to Greater China, one in particular stands out.

During a trip to New York in the early 1980s when she was running Walton Brown, Wong chanced upon a pair of *Vara* pumps, the signature bowed footwear of Italian shoemaker to the stars, Salvatore Ferragamo. Having wide feet, which made it hard for her to find suitable shoes, Wong found the *Vara* as comfortable as it was stylish.

At that time, Ferragamo had already made inroads into Hong Kong, albeit quietly, selling only the *Vara* in a store among other brands. Sensing the opportunity there, Wong did what was the most natural thing to do — for her.

"I wrote to the family and I said I would like to represent you," she recalled.

And with that, CEO Leonardo Ferragamo, son of the founder, flew to Hong Kong in 1984 to meet with her. The connection was instant but negotiations dragged on for a year before the agreement was signed.

"Leonardo was giving a speech," Wong recalled, after their working relationship was sealed. "And he said, 'We are sparring partners. While I wanted Balbina and I knew she was the right person, I had to make it tough for her because she's so good at negotiation. I was going to lose!'" she laughed. Today, Wong still maintains close ties with the second-generation Ferragamos.

Hong Kong in the 1980s had become the shopping paradise of the East but European luxury brands were largely absent. Many of these companies were family-owned and conservative in their outlook. Wong reached out to them with her charm and connections and wooed them to Asia. Apart from Ferragamo, she gathered other brands such as Cartier, Gucci, Prada, and Zegna and set them up in the first-of-its-kind luxury department store, Maison Mode.

Thanks to her, for the first time, Hongkongers got a taste of an array of European luxury on their home turf.

China calling

Many would have been satisfied with growing the business in Hong Kong. But not Wong. Another city, not too far away but far too improbable, beckoned — Shanghai.

> I could feel that this was a sleeping dragon going to wake up.

Although economic reforms in China began in 1978, it would take about 20 years before the country stepped onto the world stage. Back in the early 1990s, bicycles far outnumbered cars in Shanghai; office space was so limited it lagged behind Bangkok; and GDP per capita was a little more than US$300, compared with over US$8000 in 2016.

Against this backdrop, Wong had her job cut out for her to persuade her European principals to come on board with her to China. It all started with her instincts. "I could feel that this was a sleeping dragon going to wake up. I could also sense that the people were keen. They were eager. And I could feel there was an energy in Shanghai like I could see 40 years ago in Hong Kong," she reflected. She even managed to persuade Leonardo Ferragamo and his two brothers to visit Shanghai to feel the pulse of the city.

Still, the future was uncertain — for the brands and for Wong — as she put her reputation on the line, shouldering the responsibility of these designer labels in an untested territory. Maison Mode was set up in 1994 in Shanghai to house these brands. The store was clearly a test bed with a mere 2,700 square metres of space. Enough to showcase the brands but not too much to lose if the venture failed.

"It was not a big expense in those days to set up everybody in there. It was really trial and error," Wong said. "And it worked!"

If there is one philosophy that guides Wong's pioneering spirit, it would be going at it one arduous step at a time.

"I always believe that you don't do things altogether like opening 100 stores or 50 stores. It's always a stepping stone. Stone by stone. I started with Shanghai. Shanghai did well. I was making a little bit of money. Then, I went to the next city. And then from there I went to the second tier. From there I went to the third tier. Now, some of our brands are in the fourth-tier cities."

Her advice to those looking to go to China — be patient. "A lot of people from outside, they have had their fingers burned. They think

> I sent in my hairdressers there to cut everybody's hair to make sure they were clean and trimmed.

'China! I'm going to start 20 stores.' Don't do that. You start small and make it big," Wong advised.

And it wasn't management by remote control either. Wong didn't just oversee the partnerships, the location of the store, and the financials, she also called in the troops to help with the sales staff who were like fish out of water in the slick designer store they now had to front.

"I sent in my hairdressers there to cut everybody's hair to make sure they were clean and trimmed. They made sure they had little makeup kits, a little bit of lipstick, a little bit of cleansing cream." Down the wire, she went.

Before long, Wong would expand to Ürümqi, the remote Chinese city bordering Russia. The company then spread its wings to Taiwan and various countries in Southeast Asia. Today, ImagineX manages well-established brands like Jo Malone, Donna Karan, Paul Smith, Marc Jacobs, Tumi, Juicy Couture, Kate Spade and Tory Burch. And true to Wong's ability to spot brands, many new-to-market names have entered her stable, such as Isabel Marant, Scotch and Soda, Isaia, and Alice + Olivia.

Partnerships typically last five years and many luxury brands have Wong to thank for getting them into China. It was never meant to be a permanent arrangement and there are no hard feelings on parting and turning from partner to competitor.

"I brought them in [to China]. I was proud bringing them in. We are business people. It is inevitable," Wong said matter-of-factly. Relationships, after all, are crucial in any business. Wong should know. As much as she makes herself out to be a formidable boss, she is warm and thoughtful when it matters and that explains why many of her team members remain with her decades on — and why business associates become friends.

"We always part very well. For instance, I put Coach in China and in Hong Kong. I got the best location for them in Central — in Canton Road. And I knew it was only going to be a short term. Five years and then it was time. I'm still very good friends with the [then] CEO of Coach, Lew Frankfort. Brands come and go," Wong said.

The fact that many brands remain under ImagineX's management beyond the initial five years is noteworthy. In fact, Salvatore Ferragamo and ImagineX have moved beyond brand management to a joint venture partnership in Greater China.

The key to Wong's success is not just the instinct to know what works for the market, but it's her relationship with mall landlords throughout the region. And that, Wong believes, is what gives the company a leg-up.

She explained: "We have the best infrastructure in China for a brand that is medium-sized. It's not easy to suddenly want to infiltrate into 50 cities that I'm in. It's massive. So, they come in with us. It's about knowing all the landlords because I started with them. So, we speak with some muscle, let's put it that way."

> Unless you try it out, you don't know what is failure.

But just as there are hits, there are also misses. Wong's experience with Liz Claiborne, was one of those disappointments. The American fashion house agreed to work with ImagineX on condition the size of their stores in the US would be replicated in Asia. In 1993, Wong set up the first Liz Claiborne store in Asia in Hong Kong. She found a space for them in the heart of the city, in Times Square — all 5,000 square feet, a size unheard of in the land-scarce territory. It proved to be a costly venture doomed to fail.

On hindsight, other than the high rental incurred from the space, Wong reckoned other factors worked against Liz Claiborne's success. "It was not suitable for Hong Kong — the sizing was not right. It was a little bit, I would call it today, *mumsy*. It didn't fit in."

Wong, however, admitted her part in the failure. "I was grabbing brands. And I cannot expect that if I have 10 brands, 10 will succeed. I'll probably have one or two failures," she conceded. Not leaving it at that, Wong added, "But unless you try it out, you don't know what is failure."

The price of success

For all her achievements and occasional setbacks none compared with a personal disappointment that Wong shared openly about. The vulnerability she demonstrated midway through the interview took me a little by surprise. Here was a colourful giant of a business pioneer with a formidable presence and unsurpassed record in the industry. Yet, as open as she was about her success, she also made no bones about her dismay in sacrificing time with her daughter when she was building her career. Karthia is Wong's only child from her second marriage to a Swiss.

"One of the big sacrifices is my daughter. Putting her into boarding school at nine and seeing her, like, four times a year while I pursued my career. I was so determined. And that was a bit of a sadness for me. We kind of grew apart for a while," Wong revealed. "And going through a divorce, that was sad. Nothing would stop me in my career."

Not one to mope on the past, however, Wong quickly pointed out that mother and daughter have made up for lost time and today speak to each other on the phone every other day. Karthia lives in Switzerland where she is married with two children. "She is so proud of me," Wong beamed. "And I'm very proud of her as a mother."

Of course, Wong's two grandchildren help keep the communication going. They are apples of her eye and she speaks of them often, as a doting grandmother would. Pictures of them adorn her well-decorated office, taking pride of place on her designer furniture.

***

Having more time to herself now, Wong spends much of it in Singapore with her siblings and their families. I caught up with her again during one of her visits and at 74, her travel itinerary is still hectic by most standards. When she's not giving advice to the Group in Hong Kong for half the year, she's travelling with friends or visiting her daughter and grandchildren in Zurich.

Wong has graciously accepted that she's not as quick as she was in her 40s. She even laughs at her "senior moments."

She admits to living a charmed life. But it's more than that. It's that combination of an unrelenting drive and an uncanny ability to read people and feel the pulse of the place that has taken her to the top of her game.

What's next for her? "I think you have to go on with life. Every day, you learn," she smiled, as our conversation ended and she padded away to her next appointment in her limited edition *Vara* — at a slower pace than the last time we met four years ago, but with no less purpose.

Chapter 3

Having His Cake and Eating It

John Gokongwei Jr
JG Summit, Philippines

While many billionaires would like to be associated with their Bombardier or their Phantom as their signature mode of transport, the Philippines' second richest man on the *Forbes* list in 2017, weighing in at US$5.8 billion, has chosen a bicycle as the symbol of his ride to fame and fortune. And if a bicycle represents simplicity, diligence, and candour, then it's a befitting emblem for John Gokongwei Jr, the founder of JG Summit.

The conglomerate has businesses in airlines, food, media, hospitality, banking, petrochemicals, energy, retail and telecommunications, with a market capitalisation of over US$12 billion. You just can't go far in the Philippines without transacting with the company.

It's hard for me to forget Big John, as he's affectionately known, not only because he cuts a very imposing physical presence, but for the very inane reason that he was my first guest of the first season of *Power List Asia* in 2012! He was 86 then. And to my relief, he put my jitters to rest early on by being more thrilled than I was when we met.

Not about the interview, since he's done enough to be a veteran at it, but because he had just received, on that day, an old photograph of himself among the Chinese community in Cebu with whom he grew up. It was taken in 1940. He showed it off proudly, pointing out who's who in the restored black-and-white print that his aunt had just delivered to him. He didn't even know it existed until then.

For all that he's worth today, it's this magnate's past that seems to bring him delight and pleasure as his eyes dance over the aged print. And it wasn't even an idyllic childhood by any measure.

The beginnings

Gokongwei was born in Fujian province in China. The family migrated to Cebu to escape the unrest caused by the warlords there. It was his grandfather who owned a chain of movie houses that set the family up for a life of creature comfort.

However, wealth started to dwindle with the generations. "By the time it reached me it was zero," he said. Once again, *rags to rags in three generations* rings true.

If Gokongwei had any misgiving about his father's inability to sustain the wealth, he hid it well. He skipped a generation and credited his grandfather for passing down the entrepreneurial traits he has today. He spoke proudly of his grandfather arriving in Cebu as a migrant with little but the shirt on his back.

> I don't remember crying but I remember shock when my father died.

Gokongwei's father lived off the wealth he inherited until his death at an early age. Gokongwei was only 13 then. His father left nothing for the family. The rich kid who rode around town in a chauffeur-driven car was left to peddle around Cebu on a bicycle, hawking his wares.

Gokongwei was unflappable in the face of failures and disappointments. "Just forget it" was his mantra for dealing with defeat and pressing on. A consistent narrative that rang throughout the interview was that of a billionaire who made it "on my own."

It's hard to fault this titan for the hubris that he carries about with him. His is a story of raw and rugged hard work, of gambles he took and won, and of challenges that he didn't shy away from. No wonder he has little time for being sentimental.

The stoicism was already evident in his teenage years when his father passed away. He didn't shed a tear. "I don't remember crying but I remember shock when my father died — the shock at that moment. I don't think I cried ... I think I was too young maybe, to know how to cry, when to cry," he said.

What he did, with the help of his mother, was to pick himself up and set him and his family on a new footing. With six children, his mother could ill-afford to keep them all with her. She sent all but Gokongwei, the eldest, to relatives in China. Mother and son eked out a living initially by selling her jewellery and when the money ran out, they roasted peanuts from their backyard to sell.

When the home business proved unprofitable, young Gokongwei took to trading. The 15-year-old held his own among the 50-year-olds that he worked alongside at the *palengke*, or market, where he set up a stall. His business acumen was evident from the beginning. The teenager charted his strategy carefully, choosing first a market farther away from the centre, so that there'd be less competition, and selling items of high demand.

That meant cycling 40 kilometres to work every day and peddling soaps, threads, and candles. All these reaped a princely profit of less than US$10 daily, enough to feed the family and some to pour back into the business.

Encouraged by this venture, Gokongwei, still barely out of his teens, decided to look beyond Cebu. He began trading tyres between Cebu and Manila, travelling five days by boat and six hours by truck, one way. The business did well and Gokongwei cast his vision further.

At 20, the seasoned businessman started a trading company to import old clothes and used newspapers and magazines from the US. The business grew big enough to afford him the chance to bring his siblings back to the Philippines from China.

For all these achievements at a young age, Gokongwei summed up the principles that propelled him to success: "You realise with hard work, honesty, and perseverance, you can compete and that was I able to do as a young boy."

And competition continued to drive this tycoon, even at 86, when I met him. "My system reacts better to competition. Otherwise, you would just be sitting down at the table looking at nothing," he said.

Today as chairman emeritus, Gokongwei has taken a back seat in the operations of the business, leaving it in the hands of his youngest brother, James Go, and his son, Lance. But he's never far away from the decision-making process, as part of the executive committee. He bears down his weight when it comes to investments of more than a billion pesos (US$20 million). And nothing escapes him.

> My system reacts better to competition. Otherwise, you would just be sitting down at the table looking at nothing.

During the interview, Gokongwei drilled down to recent investments in a drugstore chain and a sugar mill and also revealed the pipeline of ideas the company had. And when I congratulated him on the recent third quarter results of Cebu Pacific, the budget airline run by his son, raking in a profit of US$55 million, at a time when airlines were going bust, he quipped, "I think should be more."

The big break

Gokongwei made his entrance into the big league at 30. Realising that trading could only churn a small profit with its thin margins, he looked to manufacturing to expand his enterprise. He started a corn starch manufacturing business in 1954. The fact that there was already a strong incumbent in Cebu that had an established name and operations did nothing to deter this young, hard-nosed businessman. While others would have shied away from the competition, Gokongwei went in head on.

"You don't think. You just believe it yourself," he said when asked what could've possessed him to take on the competition. "I did it on my own and I realised that I can compete, and I did it."

With a bank loan of US$250,000, Universal Corn Products was formed and a price war ensued. As history would tell it, Gokongwei emerged victorious. The intensity of the competition didn't just give rise to a new leader in the market but shuttered the major competitor. On this venture grew the food business that was to anchor the empire of John Gokongwei Jr.

> Small boys do not remain as small boys.

Today, Universal Robina Corporation (URC) is the largest producer and distributor of food and beverage products in the Philippines with operations throughout Southeast Asia, China, Hong Kong, Australia, and New Zealand, and markets around the world. Its top sellers are the Jack 'n Jill line of snacks and Great Taste instant coffee. Recent acquisitions include Griffin's from New Zealand and Snack Brands Australia. 2016 brought in revenue of US$2.2 billion and operating income of US$330 million.

By design or providence, the food business is the flagship of the conglomerate. His passion, his business. "I like to eat," Gokongwei said, in characteristic candour. "You see my size!"

Through the years, JG Summit has widened its reach by taking on dominant incumbents in markets that most entrepreneurs would rather avoid. Not having the first-mover advantage doesn't seem to put the Group on the back foot. Rather, they've been successful in finding niches that are untapped by existing players. They found opportunities providing budget air travel at a time when full-service Philippine Airlines ruled the Filipino skies, and they came up with innovative mobile packages through their company Sun Cellular that juggernauts such as Philippine Long Distance Telephone Co. (PLDT) and Globe hadn't thought to offer.[1]

The size of the competition does not intimidate Gokongwei. When I suggested that it was courageous of him to take on the big boys, he said matter-of-factly, "Small boys do not remain as small boys."

Never one to back down from taking on established players, Gokongwei once even accumulated enough shares in one of the most venerable of Filipino institutions, San Miguel, to qualify for a seat on the board. That was back in the 1970s when he was a little-known firebrand. In a speech he gave in 2007, Gokongwei recalled the stir he created in the business community, many of whom were opposed to this "pygmy" and were indignant of the gumption he had in taking on the establishment.[2] A legal battle ensued and Gokongwei lost. However, the battle only served to sharpen his survival instincts.

New businesses

Today JG Summit's activities revolve around seven sectors — food, real estate, power, telecommunications, banking, airlines, and

> I travel for leisure. But, in addition to that, I must have a business purpose. I cannot enjoy just leisure.

petrochemicals. The Group also has a majority stake in Singapore-listed property company United Industrial Corporation (UIC).

Several of the products in the company's stable were chanced upon during the founder's own travels. For a man always on the go, Gokongwei optimises every experience and scores with some. "I travel for leisure. But, in addition to that, I must have a business purpose. I cannot enjoy just leisure," he said. "It's good to go to museums, to plays, to the beach, but, at the same time, to look at the factories of new products. Most of the businesses are from my visits to foreign lands."

One such visit was to Massachusetts in the 1950s when he saw an advertisement for snack machines in a magazine he was flipping through while waiting in a hospital. He thought it a novel idea and made a trip to the supermarket to try it out. Six months after his visit, he brought those snack machines to the Philippines.

And so it was, too, for C2, the ready-to-drink green tea that's one of the most popular beverages in the Philippines and Vietnam. It was yet another idea that struck Gokongwei when he was in China in 2003.

He had noticed the popularity of bottled tea there and decided to change his itinerary to pay a visit to Tingyi, one of the largest food and beverage producers in China, based in Tianjin. A deal was struck. "From there I decided that the Filipinos needed something aside from Coca Cola and Pepsi Cola," he said, as if he was issuing an edict. "That's it!" he pronounced, brooking no dissent.

Today URC is run by his only son, Lance, 50, who is the heir apparent of the Group. Gokongwei holds the pre-eminent position as founder and chairman emeritus, while his brother, James Go, sits as chairman. Lance is being put through the paces to lead the conglomerate as he heads other businesses including Robinsons Land, JG Summit Petrochemical, Robinsons Retail Holdings, as well as Cebu Pacific.

If there's one business that Lance has made his own mark on, it's the Group's budget airline. It all started when Gokongwei decided one day to purchase four planes and spring a surprise on his then 30-year-old son.

> I said, 'You run this airline.' He said, 'What airline?'

"I said, 'You run this airline,'" Gokongwei recounted. "He said, 'What airline?'" And on that peremptory note Cebu Pacific came to be.

The airline was, yet again, another idea that was birthed while Gokongwei was on holiday. "I was in the US and they were talking about budget airlines, point to point. So, I took a flight on Southwest Airlines, twice. I looked at how it operated. The prices were very low. Filipinos have less income, but more islands — 7,000 islands. They want to travel from one point to another, but they have to take ships overnight. They have to get a hotel and all that. So, I decided to buy four used planes. I started the business and it worked," he explained. "So, now we are the biggest in the Philippines."

Cebu Pacific is the leading airline in the Philippines in load factor and domestic routes. It carried 19 million passengers in 2016 on its fleet of 57 planes, flying over 100 routes. It raked in a US$1.2 billion topline and registered net income of US$191 million. The success of Cebu Pacific bears testament to Gokongwei's foresight two decades earlier, of the country's pent-up demand for budget travel, and the winning gamble he took on his son; it has also become a reflection of Lance's achievement. Like father, like son.

All in the family

Throughout the interview, Gokongwei spoke of Lance with barely-contained pride. He referred to his son as "a very smart fellow," making sure to slip in his son's academic achievement — graduating summa cum laude from the Wharton School. He refuses to get drawn in to the inevitable comparisons between father and son. Gokongwei acknowledged the rules are different today than when he was running the organisation.

"Mine was a struggle for finance — how to get the money and work. And (Lance) is going to set new businesses and compete. He is in the big league now. So, it's a different kind of competition," he said.

Lance is Gokongwei's only son among six children. His daughters work in the various businesses in the Group. In November 2015, Gokongwei ceded 6.6% of the Group's shares amounting to over US$630 million.[3] Lance acquired over US$220 million of the shares, upping his stake in the Group to 7.6% while Gokongwei relinquished his share of the conglomerate to 2.8%. Robina, his daughter, has reportedly acquired some of the shares and increased her stake in the company to 2.5%. She and Lance are the only ones of Gokongwei's children who sit on the board of the Group.

> I'd rather not have in-laws in the business.

Succession is an issue that Gokongwei is unwilling to reveal much. When I asked how he decides who to give how much to, he declined to address it, saying it was an issue he'd rather not make public.

However, he is known to keep in-laws out of the family business. When I asked him about the practice, he proved, once again, evasive.

"Really there's no reason. But I'd rather not have in-laws in the business," he said.

"Even if they're competent?" I probed.

He gave a perfunctory nod.

At a forum in 2012, Lance provided an insight to the family's no-in-laws policy. It was a practice, he revealed, borne out of lessons from the past when the involvement of the extended family proved messy.

"There were situations where some of the marriages did not work. Loyalties change. Sometimes relationships between the different in-laws from the second generation become strained. Feelings get hurt. It is tricky deciding which in-law is more deserving, which is smarter, which would do a better job," he said.[4]

Succession must be a subject dear to Gokongwei's heart since he had to suffer the ignominy and hardship of generational wealth stripped from him. With the people and processes put in place, the patriarch relinquished the day-to-day operations in 2006.

"I was 80. I accepted age comes to everybody and you have to realise it's part of your life. So, that's it. You are retired; I gave the rank to the young people," he said. "It's good to see when you are alive how they are doing."

And it must be particularly good when they are doing well.

The one position Gokongwei would probably not relinquish in his lifetime is chairman of his charity, the Gokongwei Brothers Foundation, where he has pledged half his wealth to improve education in the country. He has given more than US$600 million to his foundation, making it the biggest philanthropic endowment in the Philippines.

You'd think that money has lost its hold on the man, but he was quick to point out, unapologetically, "Money is important to everybody, including the church. So, it's also important to me." Then, he promptly qualified, "But not the most important. Most important is family."

Playing devil's advocate, I probed, "Between money and family?"

"I'd rather choose family," he said, before adding a rejoinder, "But I don't want to choose. I want them both. Having the pie and eating it!" A reflection of a titan who would never cede ground, as far as he can help it.

John Gokongwei Jr certainly doesn't stray too far from his passion — and his convictions. He's come full circle, from riches to rags to riches. He's a man assured of his place in the world — then, as an audacious youngster who challenged the bigwigs and won, and now, as a patriarch of an empire that touches the lives of millions across the world.

Notes

1 PLDT, the Philippines' largest fixed network provider, has since bought a majority stake in Sun Cellular's parent company Digitel, while JG Summit holds a 12% stake in PLDT.

2 "John Gokongwei's speech at the 20th ad congress", Universal Robina Corporation, 21 November 2007, <http://www.universalrobina.com/2008/01/12/john-gokongwei-speech-at-the-20th-ad-congress/>

3 Doris Dumlao-Abadilla, "Gokongwei cedes P32B shares to heirs", Inquirer Net, 2 November 2015, <http://business.inquirer.net/201876/gokongwei-cedes-p32b-shares-to-heirs>

4 Mary Ann LI Reyes, "10 Commandments of the Gokongweis", Philstar Global, 13 March 2012, <http://www.philstar.com/headlines/786258/10-commandments-gokongweis>

Part II

SUCCESSION

E very business that is worth passing on is often stuck in a conundrum — pass on executive powers to family or professionals? Unlike European businesses that have generations of history behind them, succession in Asian businesses are a relatively new phenomenon. The exception to the rule is Japan, where family businesses may go back 20 generations.[1] The acceleration of industrialisation that took place in the 19th century during the Meiji Restoration sealed Japan's place in global business.

Outside of Japan, however, old family businesses hail largely from Europe and many trace their roots to the Industrial Revolution of the 17th century.

As for the rest of Asia, migration patterns in the early 20th century and the lack of stable political and economic structures in the past disrupted early ventures, which led to their early demise. According to the Economist Intelligence Unit, 60% of listed companies in Southeast Asia are family owned and most of them are run by the first generation.[2]

My own experience with the guests on my show over six seasons mirrors the statistics. Apart from the Zobels of the Philippines, every other tycoon I've interviewed can only lay claim to, at most, three generations of family members running the company. Being companies whose assets are in the hundreds of millions and even past a billion, naturally, the question of succession always arises and the responses have ranged from all-out certainty that children will take over the company to a definitive passing of the baton to professionals capable of taking the business to the next lap.

Leaving the operations to professional managers is a pragmatic alternative when business owners are faced with the reality that their children are incapable of leading or uninterested to run the organisation. However, that magnanimity has a short leash when the strings of the professional CEOs are pulled by board members or a family council where the owners have significant leverage on the decision-making process. So, regardless of whether a professional or a family member takes the executive reins, the DNA and values of the family will resonate through the organisation for as long as ownership remains in their hands.

The personalities featured here are unique in being a part of family businesses with a history of at least 60 years. Some have been intentional in setting up their next generation for the next phase of the company's growth, while others have been adamant, at least initially, in handing the reins to professionals. Most, however, adopt a pragmatic approach to succession.

Recognising the increasing complexity of the business landscape and the public accountability that comes with being listed, many patriarchs acknowledge that their children may not be the best equipped to run the show. Nevertheless, no one can fault them for trying. It's common practice for their children, when they do join the business, to start from the bottom like everyone else, supposedly with no special privileges and promises. Others encourage the next generation to seek employment outside of the company to gain exposure and knowledge before returning to the fold with their contributions. It's almost politically incorrect to put scions at the top, or near it, with very little experience and maturity from the start. The governance of public companies also ensures that such movements are scrutinised and very often discouraged.

Oft-cited statistics on family businesses reveal that 30% of businesses survive into the second generation, while only 12% get handed to the third. The number falls alarmingly low — to 3% — for those businesses that are run by the fourth generation.[3] These are worrying facts for family businesses and certainly would engender much deliberation in succession planning and business continuity.

Note: Naming conventions have been upended in this section in referring to individuals by their first names. This is to avoid confusion that shared family names will cause.

Chapter 4

Succession to a Tee after Seven Generations

Jaime Augusto Zobel de Ayala

Ayala Corporation

 One family that has excelled in the business of succession is the Zobels of the Philippines, for the fact that their lineage is as long as their fortunes are wide. The family owns the majority of Ayala Corporation, the oldest conglomerate in the country, stretching all the way back to 1834, tracing its roots to Spanish landowners. Today, the seventh generation is running the company, with the eighth just off the starting blocks.

With a market capitalisation of US$10 billion, the organisation's interests include real estate, utilities, telecommunications, infrastructure, retail, hospitality, construction, and banking — 11 sectors at last count. Anywhere you go in Manila, you're bound to walk into something they own. And with more than 180

> I take great pride that the Ayala that you see today is one where succession is very important to our organisation.

years of corporate history, the company has succession planning down to a tee.

"I take great pride that the Ayala that you see today is one where succession is very important to our organization," says CEO and chairman of Ayala Corporation and seventh-generation leader Jaime Augusto Zobel de Ayala, when I met him in Manila.

Jaza, as he's more fondly known by his initials, is the eldest of seven children of Jaime Zobel de Ayala, who retired as president in 1994 at the age of 60. The elder Zobel, more popularly known as Don Jaime, remained chairman until 2006 and is chairman emeritus today.

My interview with Jaza was long in coming. I had pursued him for more than a year, getting in touch with him personally after an introduction from a mutual contact. Every email written to him was promptly responded to — personally — a fact that cannot be missed when communication with the media is often left to the respective department in large organisations.

On meeting him face to face for the first time, right off the bat, Jaza apologised for the delay in scheduling the interview. It was hard to hold anything against his obvious charm. Jaza is an engaging speaker with a ready smile. He's frank (finding the company of social entrepreneurs "more interesting" than those he meets for business) and playful ("we must rejoice," he said, over the Philippines' improvement in standing in the World Bank's Ease of Doing Business rankings, even though it still hovered at the bottom half of the table).

Jaza credits his ability to run the show at Ayala in the early years, together with his brother and COO, Fernando, to his father's willingness to relinquish his executive authority — one indication of how this family has ensured a disciplined approach to succession.

"He has a clear marker and delineation of where authority should start and end," explained Jaza of his father's *modus operandi*. "And I think that's helped Fernando and I a lot. He made that very clear, and it's helped us build our own credibility and so people know that the buck stops with Fernando and I."

Nevertheless, Don Jaime, as the patriarch, had to have the last word. "He made a joke when he retired," Jaza recounted. "He said, 'I relinquish the position of the CEO of Ayala but in all other matters I remain Head of State.' Made us all laugh."

Jaza continued, "He's been a very strong figurehead. He doesn't want to play as much of a role anymore on the executive side because he doesn't want to deal with problems." In fact, the patriarch once said, " 'Deal with problems. If there's good news, come see me,' " Jaza reported, with a laugh.

Jokes aside, Don Jaime still holds the keys as head of the family council that presides over major decisions. However, it is clear that he has ceded his executive role and the fortunes of Ayala have rested on his sons since.

Under their watch, Jaza and Fernando have overseen the expansion of Ayala Corporation into new businesses such as renewable energy, infrastructure, water plants, and contactless payment, while growing existing verticals. Since Jaza took over chairmanship of Ayala Corporation in 2006, revenue has jumped threefold from US$1.4 billion to US$4.2 billion in 2016.

The Zobels present themselves as a close-knit family. They are often seen together at social and work gatherings, lending support to one another. Jaza claimed he's never had serious disagreements with his brother on major issues. Their offices are across from each other and they make sure that one is always in town when the other is travelling. Family gatherings are commonplace and probably the glue that keeps them together. The regard that the brothers have for each other is evident in my conversation with Jaza and other media interviews they've done where both would invariably offer insights into their shared roles.

Family dynamics

The onboarding of Jaza and Fernando, into Ayala Corporation is the story of the reluctant descendants who had to be persuaded to return by the patriarch.

"They didn't want to work in Ayala," revealed Don Jaime in a corporate video commemorating his retirement. "I was telling my wife, 'I've given them too much independence. I think I'm losing them.' I called them back and I said, 'Look, come back for a year. Choose your field. Find out what Ayala is all about. Not as leaders but as line people. And if you find it exciting and you think that you would like to spend your time, you're more than welcome, because I'm alone here.' They never left."[4]

Apart from the board of directors, Ayala Corporation is presided over by a family council. The Group is majority-owned by the family, through holding company Mermac Inc., named after Jaza's grand-aunt and former matriarch of the family, Mercedes Zobel McMicking. Until her death in 2005, she oversaw the family and business interests. Her portrait takes pride of place in the boardroom of the company together with her husband, Joseph McMicking, who was the mastermind behind the development of Makati in the 1950s. Today, Makati is one of the sixteen cities that make up Metro Manila and is the designated financial centre.

Jaza paid tribute to the visionary that Joseph McMicking was, pointing out the role of in-laws in the company. "He married into the family, but yet played an important role. Fundamentally, he was completely dedicated to the family, even though he had married in," Jaza said. "Until his dying day, he did everything to preserve the unity of Ayala, the unity of the family. He worked hard at it with my grand-aunt Mercedes."

> But now, this generation, we are a close family at our sibling level.

It was Mercedes, being a direct descendant, who was the matriarch and kingmaker. Being without children of her own, she appointed her nephew, Enrique Zobel to head Ayala Corporation as its first CEO in 1967 upon the corporatisation of the company. But she was also the one who removed him when he sold his 19% share of San Miguel Corporation, a company that had been in the family since its inception in 1890. Her displeasure with Enrique saw the appointment of her other nephew Jaime Zobel, or Don Jaime, to the top post.[5]

It is unrealistic to imagine family dynasties without their accompanying controversies. The challenge is to keep family ties separate from the business, or even better, nurture it and make it an asset to the company. And this, the current generation of Zobels seems to have accomplished.

"We've had our ups and downs, we've had some family issues over the years, it hasn't been perfect sailing," Jaza conceded. "But now, this generation, we are a close family at our sibling level. I have five sisters and we all get on well, thankfully. There's a lot of trust. Fernando and I communicate a lot with them. We communicate a lot with my parents.

We talk through the value structures we believe in fundamentally, rather than specific strategies of the company, and we seek alignment regularly. We make sure that we keep them informed."

The Ayala succession model

Major decisions at Ayala Corporation are made at the family council and proceed to the board of directors. And so, what is presented at the executive level gets executed on the basis of values that the family holds dear. Decisions on executive succession are no different.

"There are many times where I get asked, 'That executive is doing so well, why are you transitioning that person out?' Once you hit the 60–65-age level, it doesn't matter how effective you are, if you don't manage succession, and encourage it, and push it, then you're not creating the driver that creates longevity. And the same thing for our family. Traditionally, our family has ended up transitioning out of leadership from 60 onwards. It's just part and parcel of our belief that organisations have to renew themselves, you renew them by bringing new leadership in."

Leadership at the executive level is something the Zobel brothers take very seriously. They've kept their fingers on the pulse of current trends. In the past, even as recently as in the time of Don Jaime, the Rule of 80 was enforced. This rule adds the years of service to the age of the executive. The sum total of 80 determines the employee's retirement.

"It was our way — in the Ayala of the past, which was a little bit slower, a little more bound by family dynamics rather than professional dynamics — of encouraging movement in the company and succession. That's no longer needed. The Rule of 80 actually came to an end a little while back. There are still some that can fulfil that, we can't take it away from anyone who had it. We've kind of evolved our way out of it, and just have normal retirement programs from 60 onwards."

Innovation, new ways of doing things, fresh thinking... all part and parcel of good succession plans.

Executive positions are scrutinised yearly from the CEO down. Jaza and Fernando would look at personnel three levels down in the different companies in the Group. And executives, too, are obliged to look at the next three levels below them. In this way, they're never caught in a position of vacancy — even at the CEO level — at any time.

"And we make sure that succession deadlines are clear, well in advance, we have plans for them… and hopefully we make it a core strength of who we are as an institution. Transitions are part and parcel of any institution that aspires towards longevity. Innovation, new ways of doing things, fresh thinking… all part and parcel of good succession plans," Jaza said. "And so, we consider it a core strength, and I think we've tended to be quite good at it."

> Perhaps there might be a day in the future where the family plays a role in governance but perhaps not in the executive side.

Jaza recognised the family cannot grow faster than the organisation and so having non-Ayalas running the show is a possibility that they have to concede. "We have Ayala Corporation as a holding company, we have different operations and all those different subsidiaries are already run by professional CEOs. Fernando and I play a role as Chairman and Vice-Chairman on the governance side. Ayala Corporation is still majority-owned by our family, so there has been a strong role the family has played in the CEO role. Perhaps there might be a day in the future where the family plays a role in governance but perhaps not in the executive side," Jaza said.

"Leadership on the family side tends to move a lot more slowly than it does on the professional side. I think no institution can grow and be relevant and keep progressing if it only has family members running everything. And it's just almost impossible mathematically, genetically, and on all fronts. But there's no reason a family cannot continue a role on the governance side: have a strong role in picking the CEO, have a strong role in the values, strategy, structure. That could evolve into that in the future. Who knows?"

And the likelihood of the next generation of Zobels leading Ayala, at least immediately after Jaza and Fernando step down, is slim. Jaza will be 60 in 2019. If he were to relinquish his position at that age, as his father did, it's unlikely that the next generation would be ready to take the reins. Mariana, his eldest daughter joined the company in 2013 as an analyst before moving on to a subsidiary of Ayala Land as a senior project executive. Her latest rotation is Ayala Malls as its general manager.

By 2019, she would've just inched her way into her 30s and would not have sufficient experience to take on the top post. As a Harvard University and JP Morgan alumnus, her qualifications are certainly not in question. But the breadth and depth of the Ayala Group's businesses would require a chief executive with sufficient chops to lead it through vast organisational structures and long-term strategies and growth, not forgetting the agility and wherewithal to manoeuvre through the political landscape of the country.

Interestingly, Mariana's recent marriage to a scion of another family empire, the Aboitiz, adds another dimension to succession at Ayala. Danel, her husband, is a fifth-generation Aboitiz involved in the conglomerate that runs power, banking, food, and real estate businesses centred largely in Cebu. Seeing the opportunities as they are presented, the two companies have already formed tie-ups in real estate and construction. The marriage can only strengthen Ayala.

Jaza's only son, Jaime Alfonso, also an alumnus of Harvard University, followed his elder sister's footsteps in gaining some work experience outside of Ayala, at Goldman Sachs in Singapore. He recently returned to Manila to take on the post of brand manager at Ayala's Globe Telecom. Meanwhile younger sister, Eugenia, is a recent graduate of Brown University and works at an advertising agency in New York. The youngest, Mercedes, is still in school.

In a conversation off-camera, I teasingly asked Jaza what carrots he had to dangle to persuade Mariana to return from the US. He smiled and recalled his advice to his daughter: she could continue at JP Morgan and be just another executive there or return to Ayala and be in a position to make a significant difference. She obviously chose well.

Also on board at Ayala is Jaza's nephew, Jaime Urquijo, the son of Jaza's sister, Bea Jr. He joined the Group in 2013 at the same time as Mariana. He's on his third rotation through the corporation and is now a manager at the headquarters. Youth and inexperience also stack up against him for the top post — for now.

Indeed, only time will tell if the next generation of Zobels are worthy to assume the mantle of this venerable Filipino institution. With succession already in progress in the executive roles and governance firmly in the hands of the family, the longevity of the company is further assured for yet another generation, at least.

Notes

1 The longest surviving family business in the world hails from the Awazu Onsen district off the northwest coast of Japan. Founded in 718, the inn, Hoshi Ryokan, is run by the 46th generation today.

2 "Building Legacies: Family Business Succession in South-east Asia" The Economist Intelligence Unit, 2014, accessed 27 July 2017, <https://www.labuanibfc.com/clients/Labuan_IB-FC_78C2FF81-703A-4CAA-8926-A348A3C91057/contentms/img/resource_centre/publication/download/Building-Legacies-Family-Business-Succession-in-Southeast-Asia.pdf>

3 "Cited Stats" Family Business Alliance, accessed 12 July 2017, <http://www.fbagr.org/resources/cited-stats/>

4 "2006 Ayala Corporate Video: A Tribute to Jaime Zobel de Ayala," YouTube video, 12:20, 15 May 2011, <https://www.youtube.com/watch?v=1auHMzl9nQs>

5 Evelyn Macairan & Marichu Villanueva, "Enrique Zobel, Ayala Founder, 77", The Philippine Star, 18 May 2004.

Chapter 5

The Best Man for the Job

Roger Lee
TAL Group, Hong Kong

As one of the largest garment manufacturers in the world, TAL often spout the statistic that one in six dress shirts in the US is made by them. That's about 55 million shirts a year translated to more than US$800 million in revenue. They churn out shirts for the big names such as Burberry, Michael Kors, Brooks Brothers, and JC Penny. Management often tout themselves as "innofacturers," calling on their strong R&D roots that have produced wrinkle-free shirts and sweat-stain-proof garments. The company has 25,000 workers on their payroll, a majority of them in China.

With 70 years under its belt, TAL is run by the third generation today. While ownership of the company is in the hands of the founding family, executive leadership has, in two succession exercises, been given over to extended family members. All this while the founding family remains in various executive positions behind the CEO. Pragmatism, mutual respect and clarity of roles keep the management arrangement in harmonious balance.

TAL Group began business in Shanghai in 1946 as a textile mill. Its founder, CC Lee, fortuitously set up shop in Hong Kong in the 1950s after the machines he ordered from the US were barred from entering China because of licensing issues. Hong Kong seemed the most obvious place to offload them. Other textile operators from the mainland also found themselves in a similar predicament and so began the rise of the textile industry that Hong Kong would become known for. This was dominated by migrants from Shanghai and Chaozhou fleeing the Communist stranglehold on their businesses.

In the 1960s, after CC Lee had relocated the business to Hong Kong, he was hit by another restriction. This time, the US quota system, which limited textile imports from Hong Kong and Japan. This forced him to set up factories outside of Hong Kong just to reach their major market. Factories were established in Thailand, Malaysia and Taiwan. As wages in Hong Kong began to rise, management was forced to face the ghost of their past — China. In 1995, TAL bit the bullet and returned to China to take advantage of the lower labour costs.

In looking for a successor, CC Lee set his eyes on his nephew, Harry Lee, even though his two sons, Richard and George, had been involved in the business for over a decade by then. Harry was an unlikely candidate for the top post. He studied engineering in the UK and later pursued a doctorate in Brown University in the US. He was more suited for a life in academia.

When Harry returned to Hong Kong for what he believed would be a vacation, CC Lee coaxed him to stay on and, shortly after, dispatched him to Malaysia to run the factory there. That was in 1979. Harry became managing director four years later. CC Lee's son, Richard, was made chairman.

From the second to the third

For 30 years, Harry Lee had grown the business despite the challenges from the booms and busts of economic cycles. He steered the company through a series of buyouts and brought back ownership entirely into the family's hands. Harry also put his engineering bent to good use, developing high-quality materials while focusing on efficiency in the supply chain. When it came time to hand over the reins, he made an emphatic decision to turn to recruitment specialists, in search of the next generation of leaders.

I met with Harry Lee at the company's factory in Dongguan in the Pearl River Delta in 2014. He was there to mark the facility's 20th anniversary with a banquet thrown for all 4,000 workers there. Tables filled every square inch of the factory compound with the usual fanfare of speeches, animated emcees, blaring music, and cheongsam-clad ushers. Harry carried the official title of Chairman and the unofficial one of Chief R&D Officer. At 72, he still reported for work every day.

Harry recalled the occasion when his son and current CEO, Roger Lee, broached the subject of joining the company. "When he graduated, he asked me, 'What's the possibility of coming back to the company?' I said, 'Zero.'"

Not surprising if you were to consider the way Harry raised his son. I met Roger in 2014 when he was 40 years old and two years into the top job. According to him, he was groomed to be more of a scientist than a scion.

"When I was growing up," Roger recounted, "my father being who he is, a scientist and an engineer, would always quiz me about things; take things apart, ask me to put it back together, that kind of engineering training. Did I come to work with him sometimes? Yes. I played tennis with some of his customers? Absolutely, yes. So, I had that kind of exposure. But to me, it's not groomed me to be someone running a company because we never talked about that."

And since the apple doesn't fall far from the tree, Roger went on to follow his father's footsteps with an engineering degree in the UK. Later, armed with an MBA from Imperial College London, he joined an IT consultancy in the US for nine years. The time away from the business, he believes, was a vital part of his preparation for his position at TAL. Not for the specifics of the job but for the taste of the real world and the benefits that come with tough love.

> When he graduated, he asked me, 'What's the possibility of coming back to the company?' I said, 'Zero.'

"You have to be working outside to gain the experience," he said. "People would tell you exactly what's on their mind, what is right or wrong. You have good bosses, you have bad bosses. You learn a lot outside. Whereas, when you're a family member, you won't. People won't tell you the stuff that you need to know to get better," he said.

Comparing his experience working without and within TAL has given Roger an invaluable perspective. "Even when I started at a lower level (at TAL), nobody would tell me off because they're afraid of who my father was. And that doesn't work because the only way you get better is to learn from mistakes. And when you don't know you're making a mistake because no one tells you, you're not going to get better. So, I believe if I started day one in this company, out of my Masters, I won't be able to run the company today," he said.

> You learn a lot outside. Whereas, when you're a family member, you won't. People won't tell you the stuff that you need to know to get better.

In a study by consulting firm Ernst & Young, 75% of the 1000 family businesses surveyed insist family members seek employment outside of the family concern for between two and five years.[1] The experience the successors bring, undoubtedly widens options and strategies for the family business. It also makes for more well-rounded leaders.

When Roger finally returned to Hong Kong to join TAL in 2005, he received no special treatment nor promise of the top post. It was with reluctance that Harry called on both Roger and Delman Lee, CC Lee's grandson, to return home to the family business.

"I wanted to have an outside professional to run the company," revealed Harry. "So, I tried about five years to get some headhunters to try to help me find the successor. And we found two candidates. One stayed on for a few months, and he left. The second one stayed on but I felt that he's probably not the right person. And by that time, it was already five years. So, I decided to try to get [Roger and Delman] to come back."

Typically, scions are expected to learn the ropes from the ground up. And so it was for Roger, making his rounds in sales, production, operations, and human resource. He even spent a few years in the factory in Malaysia, like his father.

It was a seven-year climb to the top and Roger's appointment as CEO was decided by a professional executive committee, with the blessing of the founding family. Harry Lee was 70 when he handed over the reins, about the same age when CC Lee retired.

In my conversation with both Harry and Roger, there would invariably be an acknowledgement that while they are a part of a family concern, they don't own the business. That honour belongs to Delman, who is the Chief Technology Officer and Vice Chairman. Ownership is in his and, his father, Richard's hands. Richard is now honorary chairman, while Harry is chairman. Delman holds a doctorate in electrical engineering from Oxford University and worked as a researcher in the US and the UK until 2000 when he returned to Hong Kong and joined the family business.

In an interview with Forbes, Delman described the roles he and Roger play. "On day-to-day issues, I report to Roger; on the other side, he reports to me, the owner," Delman said. "It's a very good balance."[2]

Delman had reportedly conceded early on that he was not cut out for the leadership role. "I am not a suitable candidate. I am not a good salesperson, not outgoing. I am quiet."[3]

> I always believe that a business, to be successful, must have the best person in the job. And that doesn't have to be a family member.

In this family business, the focus is clearly placed on the best people for the job and, not necessarily, the rightful ones. And it seems the families are in agreement on what it takes to lead TAL into the future. The pipeline of talent within the family is pointing in a clear direction. "I believe the next person that's going to take over from my position will not be a family member," said Roger. "I always believe that a business, to be successful, must have the best person in the job. And that doesn't have to be a family member. Family members help in terms of carrying on the tradition but any other person can also believe in the tradition, believe in the DNA, and do an equally, if not, better job."

Curiously, for all the company has done to ensure promotion by merit, Roger's family ties are an inadvertent thorn in the flesh that haunts him now and again. "You sometimes think, are you at the position you're at because of who you are, because you're related to the family, because your father ran it? Or because you're really and truly competent. Sometimes that creeps in," concedes Roger.

"Having self-doubt, you know, because of who you are, that will never go away because of the history," he mused.

Notes

1 "In harmony: Family business cohesion and profitability", Ernst & Young & Kennesaw State University, accessed 12 July 2017, <http://www.ey.com/Publication/vwLUAssets/Family_business_cohesion_and_profitability/$FILE/EYFamilybusinesscohesionprofitability.pdf>

2 Shu-Ching Jean Chen, "Staying Close To Roots, Lees Of Hong Kong Restored A Garment Leader", Forbes Asia, 21 November 2016.

3 Shu-Ching Jean Chen, as above.

Chapter 6

Bollywood or Business?

Anand Mahindra
Mahindra & Mahindra, India

Anand Mahindra was appointed to the top executive post in one of India's leading industrial houses in 1997, some 16 years after he took on an obscure position as Executive Assistant to the Finance Director in one of the Group's businesses, Mahindra Ugine Steel. Finding his fit in the conglomerate entailed breakthroughs and breakdowns. While he was celebrated as the man behind the iconic Indian sports utility vehicle, the Scorpio, he had also nearly lost his life for introducing unpopular measures in a plant.[1]

Today, Mahindra & Mahindra is one of India's largest conglomerates, raking in revenue of US$17.8 billion in 2016 from businesses ranging from defence and automobiles to travel and IT services spread across 100 countries. Formed in 1945, the company started off in the steel business and became known for importing the iconic Willys Jeep to India. Anand is the third generation Mahindra to run the company and holds the position of Executive Chairman of the Group.

I met him in 2014 at his office in Mumbai, in a heritage building a stone's throw from the historical Gateway of India. He cut a dapper image of sophistication, used to being in the public eye. He was articulate and sharp and noticeably as comfortable in front of the camera as he was behind it. He did, after all, graduate magna cum laude from Harvard in film studies. (Anand jokingly remarked that he had "to atone for those sins" of studying film, by going on to do his MBA at Harvard.)

Other than the Scorpio, Anand also launched other businesses in the Group like real estate and hospitality while overseeing high-profile acquisitions such as SsangYong Motor, Satyam Computer Services (now Mahindra Satyam), and Reva Electric Car Company (now Mahindra Reva Electric Vehicles). He is a much sought-after thought leader in his country and has made good use of social media to reach his 6.5 million followers on Twitter.

According to popular belief, business dynasties groom their children from a young age to take over the family business. There are dramatic portrayals of scions compelled to learn the ropes and take on fields of study they are not inclined to. This perception, however, holds no sway with the Mahindras. Anand himself was given leeway to indulge in his love for film. His uncle, Keshub Mahindra, who handed the reins of chairmanship to Anand, has three daughters who are not involved with the Group. Nor are Anand's two daughters, who have followed the family's love of the arts.

"Their skills and competencies are in another direction which I would call the true family business and that is, they're both designers," declared Anand, proudly. "They're both creative people. One of them is a graphic designer in New York and she's designing the logo of our new film company. And the other one is a wannabe filmmaker and writer. So, she writes for my wife's magazine called *IQ*. She's written some wonderful think pieces over there and, let's see, she'll probably want to make a movie at some point in time, making me the producer and making life come full circle again."

For the Mahindras, being a part of the family business has been an option and not a predisposition. Only the willing and able may throw in their lot, leaving those who have different callings unencumbered by the legacy. It is this latitude and magnanimity that has been a boon to Anand's own approach to the business. He recalled an occasion after the successful launch of the Scorpio when he was approached by a member of the board with a surprising revelation. Unknown to him, throughout the development phase of the Scorpio — the most expensive project the company had ever undertaken at US$110 million — the directors had decided among themselves that if the project were to fail, it would be Anand's head on the chopping block.

"Thank God I never knew that because I probably would have been scared out of my skin and never would have had the courage to do it!" he revealed.

Anand drew parallels from that situation where he was unwittingly free of pressure that would've paralysed him, to the freedom he's been given by his family to pursue his options. "When I look back, if you are not fearing the absence of a job, if you know you will find work to do and have an alternate career, if every decision you make at work is not something about 'Oh my God! I'm going to lose my job and my livelihood,' then you make better decisions," he said.

> It's less about me being a family member, more about my saying, 'Well I have nothing to lose; I'm going to do what's right.'

"So, it's less about me being a family member, more about my saying, 'Well I have nothing to lose; I'm going to do what's right.' Because if it doesn't work out, that's fine. I've got other things I can do and other talents I can pursue. I think that's very key in a lot of the decisions I've been making over the last couple of decades," Anand said.

Succession programmes

It appears that Anand is the last of the Mahindras for a long time yet to take on the key executive post in the corporation. Succession planning has been focused outside of the family. "I succeeded a professional as managing director, somebody who had been managing director for almost 15–20 years. And so, this company has seen professionals leading it and this company knows that a professional will lead this in the next cycle because my daughters don't want to be in the business. They have their own careers to make. I don't have any cousins or nephews or anyone else in the family. So, there will be a professional who will succeed me", Anand said emphatically.

In 2016, Anand relinquished his post of managing director to long-time employee Pawan Goenka, while he took on executive chairmanship. Anand will take on an oversight role and both his and Goenka's posts will be up for review when both turn 65 in 2020. That's the retirement age for executive positions in the group. It is likely that

> This company has seen professionals leading it and this company knows that a professional will lead this in the next cycle because my daughters don't want to be in the business.

Anand will continue to exert influence on the Group's decisions as chairman, but the operations of the conglomerate will be helmed by an outsider for years to come.

Seeing this foregone conclusion, the company has put various succession plans in place. In 2010, a decade before Anand's impending retirement, it almost tripled its executive board from eight to 23 members, bringing in not just the heads of the business units but also the level below. This reflects the company's stance of taking leadership renewal and expansion to a level that will match the breadth of the Group's business.[2] It's also a pragmatic move when the original board was made up of presidents in their 50s and 60s. New leadership programmes, with a younger cohort, serve as the pipeline of talent among the 40,000 employees in the Group.

While traditionalists may bemoan the end of an era of executive leadership among the Mahindras, it's unlikely that the family would be too wistful about the handover. With the company's track record of countless professional heads in years past and its robust succession plan, the Group looks set to forge ahead to the next level.

And no prizes for guessing what Anand would do if he didn't have a multibillion dollar conglomerate to run.

"I'd be behind the camera making a film," he said, as his eyes lit up. Bollywood awaits.

Notes

1 In 1991, Anand was holed up for four hours in his plant office after workers rose in protest against his announcement that Diwali bonuses would no longer be an entitlement but, instead, would be tied to productivity. Anand had described the incident as "violent" and "threatening" and had even called his wife during that time "almost to say goodbye".

2 From the Mahindra Group's press release: "Mahindra Group announces changes in senior management", Mahindra Group, 1 April 2010, <http://www.mahindra.com/news-room/press-release/1294035199>

Part III

EAST GOES WEST

The western market, a frontier made up of North America and Western Europe, has traditionally been impenetrable by outsiders, particularly Asians brands. The exceptions are products from Japan, thanks to early industrialisation that began during the Meiji Restoration in the mid-19th to early 20th century and accelerated after World War II.

Even the rise of the Asian Tigers of Singapore, Hong Kong, South Korea, and Taiwan from the 1960s and of China from the 1980s was premised on the resources these countries provided as OEMs (Original Equipment Manufacturers). Brand Asia still lacked credibility in the eyes of the West. Acquisition proposals from Asian conglomerates eyeing western businesses invariably faced political, economic, and social opposition.

However, with innovation and commitment, some Asian companies have broken through the ranks to be recognised as best-in-class. Slowly but surely, these organisations have won the trust of Western communities, resulting in acquisitions of business concerns that had, hitherto, been proudly local.

In this section, I highlight the journeys of three entrepreneurs who took those intrepid steps to the West by buying companies larger than themselves; taking over utilities of local communities that, for a long time, were part of a protected industry; and pitching their best products in an arena that had been an exclusive Western enclave for centuries.

All glorious breakthroughs follow fits and starts. While their paths to acclaim in the West are lessons in themselves, there are also the unglamourous struggles of pushing through radical policies and the trepidation of taking on monumental risks just to drive their companies to the doorstep of the West.

But the benefits of these audacious overtures have not just been financially rewarding for the Asian businesses, they've extended to higher operating standards at home, a wider range of skills across the board and more expansive visions for the leaders.

Chapter 7

A Prophet is Not Accepted in His Own Country

Francis Yeoh

YTL Corporation, Malaysia

I n 2014, Malaysian social media was abuzz when the managing director of one of Malaysia's largest conglomerates reportedly called for an end to crony capitalism. Francis Yeoh, the scion of the YTL empire, was widely criticised by keyboard warriors and politicians, past and present, for his challenge. Many accused him of being the very recipient of lucrative government contracts by cosying up to the powers that be back in the 1990s — the crucial period that launched YTL into the big league.

Yeoh had declared at a government forum in 2014 that 85% of his business had come from outside of Malaysia, in particular Britain, Singapore, and Australia. He was quoted as saying "The good thing about these three territories, I don't have to *kowtow* to the prime minister before I do deal(s), I don't have to see them even after I've won the deal...I turn West because of this transparent, coherent regulatory framework."[1] The report created a furore that Yeoh felt compelled to respond to a few days later. He said he was misrepresented and his point was, instead, to dispel the perception that cronyism was the way successful Malaysian businesses operated.[2]

YTL is one of Malaysia's largest conglomerates, with interests in construction, cement, real estate, utilities, hospitality, and information technology. With a market capitalisation of US$7 billion and revenue of US$3.8 billion in 2016/2017, YTL's businesses spread beyond Malaysia to Singapore, Indonesia, Australia, Jordan and the UK.

I met with Yeoh in 2013 in a suite at the Ritz-Carlton in Kuala Lumpur, which YTL owns. He was effusive and well-read. Throughout the interview, he spoke in analogies of the Faustian bargain and the Gordian knot. In fact, we were arguing over a quote, which I insisted was from Woodrow Wilson, but Yeoh begged to differ. He whipped out his smartphone to check the source of the quotation, and yours truly prevailed with a congratulatory high five from the dissenter.

Yeoh is a man who wears his heart on his sleeves. He is well-known as an evangelical Christian who peppers his conversation with the name of Jesus. (In fact, he jested that YTL, other than being the initials of his father, also stands for Yahweh, The Lord.) When he is convicted about an issue, it's hard to get a word in edgewise, like when he started on the subject of transparency in Britain, Singapore, and Australia.

He is an admirer of the British system, often lauding its policies and its leaders. "In Britain, there is a real premium transparent, coherent regulatory framework, where the rule of law is the order of the day. I think that's what counts," he said. "They don't flip-flop on policies." Post Brexit and his tune remains, as he has continued his acquisition of assets in the UK.

They don't flip-flop on policies.

Turning to Singapore, even though margins in real estate development in the island state are relatively thin, it is the predictability of operating there that attracts him. "Singapore is, at least, easy. If I've got the finance and I also have the skills, I can bid openly. I don't have to speculate whether I can win or not. I know my margins and all that. If I'm prepared to live with a lesser margin, at least I have a turnover; I have a profit; I have a project," he said.

Yeoh has been consistent on the value he places on transparency — back in 2013 when he spoke with me and later at the forum. The backlash he received from statements he made at the forum must be understood in the light of a controversial mega deal (and all the intricacies it involved) that not only was the first to be done in Malaysia, but was the launch pad that catapulted YTL to territories beyond Malaysia and into the West.

The golden goose or Pandora's box

Many mistake the YTL empire to have begun with Yeoh's late father, Yeoh Tiong Lay, because his initials are borne by the company. But the family credits Yeoh Cheng Liam of the previous generation, who began with a timber business in the 1920s, as the founding entrepreneur. When Yeoh Tiong Lay took over in the 1950s, he branched out into construction, taking advantage of Malaysia's rapid development. He made his mark with some landmark buildings in the country.

But as far as the size of projects was concerned, construction was small change compared to the maiden award of the independent power producer (IPP) license by the Malaysian government in 1993. This came about under the watch of the third generation, led by Francis Yeoh. YTL was the first private company to secure the coveted license and shortly after, launched an initial public offering which brought in a windfall of US$975 million. One year after completion of the plant, YTL's turnover ballooned to US$600 million, an almost 5-fold increase before the license was awarded.

Many, including those who joined the fray in criticising Yeoh for his statements at the forum in 2014, believed this was the golden goose that launched YTL into the international league.

To understand how YTL came to be the top contender for the license, it's worth noting that shortly before the idea of an IPP in Malaysia was mooted, the country was hit by a severe blackout in 1992. This forced the economy to a standstill for two days. It was an embarrassment to Prime Minister Mahathir Mohamad, who was flying Malaysia's flag to the world as the place where foreign investors could park their money and businesses.[3]

In Yeoh's books, it was a case of the best man for the job. When Mahathir became prime minister for the first time in 1981 (he has since been re-elected to the post in 2018), he was already 56 and that, Yeoh believed, accounted for the premier's *modus operandi*. "He was a man in a hurry. He wanted solutions and I happened to be a contractor. I was the first turnkey contractor, home-grown, to do design-and-build. So,

> If you've got a good idea and Mahathir liked it and it's good for the people, he will give you that first crack.

at that time, if the locals couldn't compete, he'd flush us all out. And he didn't care," Yeoh said.

This meant that projects had to be done well and fast. Where it used to take eight years to build a hospital, Mahathir wanted it done in a shorter time. Yeoh said of Mahathir, "He said, 'If you can compete, we give you a chance to compete.' And we were given a chance in a hospital and we did it in two years and five months. It was a record! And that, Mahathir took notice." YTL made further impressions on the country's leader with its construction of 12 government hospitals, an airport in Sarawak, and a 300-acre light industrial park.

"If you've got a good idea and (Mahathir) liked it and it's good for the people, he will give you that first crack. First come, first served. That way, he rewarded people at that time, regardless of race," Yeoh insisted, "It's the quality of the idea at that time in history."

It was Yeoh's track record, he believed, that won him the IPP license and enabled him to navigate his way through several landmines to set up an unprecedented venture.

According to him, it was a challenging undertaking. He had to negotiate with several government agencies and propose new initiatives to make the venture viable for YTL.

"I almost gave up, actually. It was so difficult to do it," he recalled.

First, there was the issue of funding. Yeoh explained, "There was no financing of a private power in its own currency. It's only done in US dollars. It was ridiculous to have the US dollar element as an intermediary when actually we are being paid in ringgit and doing services in ringgit. So, why the US dollar element, except that the experience of private power comes from the West?"

Yeoh suggested the bond should be raised in the local currency, the ringgit. The Central Bank agreed.

Then came the second breakthrough in financing history in Malaysia. Where bonds were typically issued over a period of five years, a 15-year tenor was pitched instead. Yeoh cited the country's strong budget surplus and touted long-term savings from long-term projects. The Central Bank agreed.

In order to further sweeten the deal, he persuaded the government to allow him to list YTL Power on the local bourse without the requisite 5-year track-record qualification. "I said to the authorities, our stock exchange, 'Why can't we let investors decide whether this idea of independent power is a good idea?'" Yeoh said. The Malaysian bourse agreed, and the gamble paid off handsomely, allowing the company to raise US$975 million.

Remarkably, Yeoh was very successful in his proposals to the various authorities. He insisted it was his credibility with the former premier that helped secure many of these deals because Mahathir urgently needed good people and plans. "At that time in history, Dr Mahathir was a man on a mission. He was a man of courage and he wanted change," Yeoh said.

Behind the scenes at the YTL headquarters, though, it was a harrowing time. The venture was to be all-or-nothing for the company. "You know, at that time we had to come up with all the cash YTL Corp ever had. That was our bet. We put every cash — MYR 300 million (US$116 million) — into equity. If I got it wrong, if my guys didn't do it well, or didn't know how to do it well, we would have collapsed. And, I mean, that's it. We would have gone bust! If it had been delayed by one day, hundreds of thousands would've been lost. It was extremely high-risk. But I thank God it's done well and it's great."

With the huge war chest, YTL began to look abroad for acquisitions. The timing was opportune. The company began the push overseas in 2000. It was also during that time when rumours of Mahathir's impending retirement surfaced. The premier stepped down in 2003, after 22 years in office.

> We realised that we can be a hostage geographically if we don't move out of Malaysia.

When I noted how timely his overseas ventures seemed in light of Mahathir's retirement, Yeoh responded unequivocally that it was just a prudent thing to do for the business, "We realised that we can be a hostage geographically if we don't move out of Malaysia." He added, "Mahathir was very gung-ho to open up privatisation. But, in 1997, he shrunk back and said,

'Maybe, we have to slow down on that.' But we had to go on." 1997 was the year of the Asian Financial Crisis that saw the ringgit plunge a third against the US dollar.

Interestingly, YTL managed to come out of the crisis relatively unscathed because it dealt very little in foreign exchange. It was prescient, too, that the power facility financing was pegged to the ringgit.

Venturing forth

While YTL is known to be flushed with cash, Yeoh's philosophy has always been to wait for the right price at the right point of the cycle. He said, "I can't pay today the prices people are paying for shopping centres and the returns that they get, not because my shareholders will scream at me, but I just think there will be opportunities in all cycles. There will a down cycle and, then, maybe it would be less crowded."

Getting to the rub, he revealed the key to his investment strategy. "Patience is the virtue that you must harness if you're a long-term player. And since we're long-term players, patience is quite an important commodity that we already have in our DNA."

> Patience is the virtue that you must harness if you're a long-term player.

In 2000, the company acquired 33.5% of South Australia's Electranet, a consortium of companies that manages the territory's transmission network. It was his first taste of a utility company overseas, and it whetted Yeoh's appetite for more.

When word got out that a water company in South West England was for sale, YTL threw in a bid. Wessex Water attracted the attention of other worthy suitors in the form of Hong Kong tycoon Li Ka Shing's Hutchison Whampoa, Italy's utility Enel, and a consortium led by the Royal Bank of Scotland.

Up to a week before Wessex was to announce its new owners, the RBS consortium was certain they had won. They were given the impression they were in exclusive talks with Azurix, Wessex's owner, and that YTL had dropped out of the race. RBS was even ready to offload its share of another water company since it was against the law in the UK to own more than one water business.[4] But it was not to be.

The factor that reportedly weighed against RBS was Azurix's concern that the bank would load on caveats to the deal as the owner's parent company, Enron, was heavily in debt (the American conglomerate was declared bankrupt in 2001). YTL's offer was more favourable, for not only was it slightly higher, but it enabled Azurix to "retire substantially all of our debt," according to its chairman at the time.[5]

In 2002, YTL won the bid to purchase Wessex Water in perpetuity for GBP1.24 billion (US$1.8 billion).

But the champagne couldn't be popped yet. Top of YTL's to-do list was to assure the staff that the new owners would not ride roughshod over them. One of the first policies set in place was an employee share option scheme. Depending on their salary and length of service, staff were given an average of 20,000 share options in YTL Power over three years, priced at 50p (US$0.75).[6]

> They were afraid that, like their previous owners, (we) would ask them to cut corners or squeeze profits out of every quarter.

Yeoh empathised with the workers' initial concerns. "They were afraid that, like their previous owners, (we) would ask them to cut corners or squeeze profits out of every quarter. We were not. We said, 'Hey, you're now a top 10 water company in the UK. We want to be number one. Take your time. Once you understand, we give you staff options. We're here and we will not sell. Forever.' I dare to use this term 'forever' because if it is good I will keep it forever," Yeoh said.

Next was the issue of the local community that Wessex Water served. They had not heard of the Malaysian owners until then and, in Yeoh's words, were "terrified." Being a fan of opera, Yeoh decided to calm frayed nerves with music. He pulled out all the stops in a massive public relations exercise that followed.

He called on his good friend, the late tenor Luciano Pavarotti and, for good measure, his fellow performers, who together made up the world-renowned Three Tenors. As if that wasn't enough, the singers were accompanied by the Royal Philharmonic Orchestra. The residents of Bath were feted to an outdoor concert like they had never experienced before. The event was a resounding success, "and they welcomed us as an investor," declared Yeoh.

Wessex Water has seen its profits increase over the years from US$17.5 million when YTL took over to US$215 million in 2016. At the same time, they've achieved consistently high customer satisfaction ratings from its 2.7 million consumers, even being recognised as the best performing company with the least number of complaints.[7]

Little wonder then, as residents in the area became more comfortable with the Malaysian owners, a proposal came knocking. "Because of our culture," said Yeoh, "the people of Bath welcomed us and said, 'Hey! There's this hotel, we want to give it to you.'"

Expanding further in the UK

A heritage hotel built in the 1820s was badly in need of restoration. A college had occupied it for 70 years until 2005. Prior to that, it was a hospital famed for its thermal water supplied from a neighbouring spring. It was this piece of history that YTL was offered by the council for redevelopment.

> I don't put a Malaysian CEO when I take over companies in Singapore or the UK.

YTL spent US$20 million to transform the three historical buildings into a 5-star hotel, the Gainsborough Bath Spa, which opened in 2015. The luxury accommodation has 99 guestrooms and a natural thermal spa. The water is supplied from the neighbouring Thermae Bath Spa, which was also taken over by YTL. The spa is a popular tourist destination in Bath, a city famous for its thermal water. All 170 employees kept their jobs, and the spa kept its name. The former managing director was retained as an advisor to the group's hotel unit.

Similarly, when the Malaysian company took over Wessex Water, CEO Colin Skellett, continued his tenure for what was supposed to be five years. Not only has Skillett stayed on, he's even had his portfolio expanded to include the role of Chairman of YTL's Bath Hotel & Spa & YTL Land and Property in the UK.

Yeoh is adamant about the practice of using locals to lead his businesses overseas. "I don't put a Malaysian CEO when I take over companies in Singapore or the UK," he asserted.

In the same way, only local architects and planners are involved in the development of YTL's biggest project yet in Britain. In 2015, YTL seized another opportunity, this time a massive land bank of 350 acres in Bristol, one of the most economically dynamic cities in Britain. The Filton Airstrip was the home of Concorde, the supersonic passenger jet. For an undisclosed amount, the company signed a deal to develop yet another historically significant site into a township for residential and commercial use.

YTL's credentials were cited for their success in winning the deal. Mike Craddock from BAE Systems, the aerospace company that owned the land, said, "We wanted to ensure that we chose a buyer with the skills and track record to deliver the vision for the redevelopment of this regionally important brownfield site."[8]

Not stopping there, the Group's hospitality division has acquired other properties, like a 77-room church-turned-hotel in Edinburgh, a row of five Georgian townhouses converted into a hotel in London and a quaint retreat in Berkshire.

***

After the last public outcry in Malaysia over Yeoh's statements on cronyism, YTL withdrew its participation in a US$670 million power plant in Johore, located in the southern part of Malaysia. The consortium, of which YTL was a part, secured the project through direct negotiations.

In its statement, the company said its decision to pull out of the deal was "to dispel any misgivings over the Government's commitment to transparency and good governance."[9] The company, however, said it welcomed the opportunity to work on the project in other capacities and through a competitive process. The work was eventually awarded to other partners in the consortium.[10]

In a country where business, race, and politics are intrinsically entwined, it is hard for Malaysian businessmen who've gained some modicum of success not to be viewed suspiciously. In the case of YTL, the pull factors to go West were as strong as the push factors at home.

To use a biblical reference familiar with Yeoh, a prophet is never accepted in his own country.

Many considered the glory days of YTL in Malaysia a thing of the past, particularly for its cash cow, the power business. Its 21-year power purchase agreement with the national grid expired in 2015 and, despite getting a 34-month extension, the market reacted with indifference.

But time and again, the company has proven itself nimble and resilient. Just as it gave up the project in Johore, 18 months later, it revealed plans to build a US$2.7 billion plant in Java, Indonesia, with a 30-year power purchase agreement with the country's national utility company.

Then, at the end of 2017, Yeoh announced that its construction arm had been awarded a US$2.3 billion contract to build an electrified double tracking railway project in the southern part of Malaysia, stretching almost 200 kilometers.[11] This sent its share price soaring by 30%.

As much as the Malaysian public would want to cast aspersions on YTL and its founding family, it is hard to ignore their success from the international accolades they have received as well as the quality of the work they have left their stamp on. Indeed, it's hard to ignore parallels of the legend of the Faustian Bargain, which Yeoh alluded to frequently in the interview, to the situation that he's found himself caught in at home — his phenomenal success since the 1990s in Malaysia has also been dogged by niggling suspicions. Metaphors aside, however, YTL is one of the rare enterprises that has had the gumption, endurance and foresight, to grow and stretch beyond its comfortable reach while riding the usual highs and lows of cycles that are just part of any growth story.

Notes

1 Melissa Chi, "Crony capitalism in Malaysia has to go, son of YTL founder says", 3 June 2014, Malay Mail Online, accessed 14 July 2017, <http://www.themalaymailonline.com/malaysia/article/crony-capitalism-in-malaysia-has-to-go-son-of-ytl-founder-says>

2 "Francis Yeoh says not a crony of former PM", The Star Online, 5 June 2014 <http://www.thestar.com.my/business/business-news/2014/06/05/francis-yeoh-says-not-a-crony-of-former-pm/#Re0IymWZ7YPThXJt.99>

3 Much controversy surrounds the blackout. The former executive chairman of the national grid, Tenaga Nasional Berhad (TNB), Ani Arope (the whipping boy of the incident turned whistle-blower) claimed that the power outage would not have happened if the government had allowed TNB to go ahead with its plan to build two more power plants to support the growing needs of the country. Instead, he said, these plans were handed over to private companies. ("Ani: TNB got a raw deal", 6 June 2006, The Star Online, accessed 14 July 2017, <http://www.thestar.com.my/business/business-news/2006/06/06/ani-tnb-got-a-raw-deal/>)

4 Mary Fagan, "Who the hell are YTL?", The Telegraph, 31 March 2002.

5 Eric Portanger, "YTL Power Buys Wessex Water From Enron for $776.4 Million", 26 March 2002, The Wall Street Journal.

6 Tan Kah Peng, "Wessex chief turns down Wessex share options", 26 June 2003, The Star.

7 "Delving into Water 2016: Performance of the water companies in England and Wales 2011-12 to 2015-16", November 2016, Consumer Council for Water.

8 "Filton Airfield sold for development", 7 December 2015, B24/7, accessed 14 July 2017, <https://www.bristol247.com/news-and-features/news/filton-airfield-sold-for-development/>

9 YTL News Release, 18 June 2014.

10 "TNB returns as SIPP's partner in RM4.7bil power project", The Star Online, 3 May 2017 <https://www.thestar.com.my/business/business-news/2017/05/03/tnb-takes-majority-stake-in-rm4pt7bil-power-project-in-johor/#RTKv27zR4tLXcAHu.99>

11 "YTL Corp's order book expected to balloon with Gemas-JB rail project, say analysts", The Edge Markets, 14 December 2017.

Chapter 8

Pacing with the Best

Tony Lo
Giant Bicycles, Taiwan

T he Tour de France is not just a showcase of the human spirit —
known to be one of the most gruelling races in the world, with
21 day-long stages, over more than 3,500 kilometres — it's also
a beauty parade where bike enthusiasts gather to gawk at the most
sophisticated and advanced bicycles fresh off the factory floor.

Among the brands proudly represented, there are the usual
suspects of European and North American marques, like Specialized,
Trek, Canyon, Cervelo, Lapierre, and Pinarello. Also, a regular in the
Tour since 1997 is the brand that has earned its stripes not just as a
maker of high-performance bicycles but as the biggest earner, with
US$1.9 billion in sales in 2016. It likes to be called "a global company;
it just happens that the headquarters is in Taiwan," so says the former
CEO of Giant Bicycles.

Tony Lo is as synonymous with Giant Bicycles as its founder,
King Liu. The pair formed a formidable partnership in 1972 when
Lo joined Liu a year after the company was formed. They played
very distinct roles in the organisation with Liu overseeing the
technical aspects of the business, while Lo did the marketing. Lo's
command of English made him the face of Giant Bicycles in the
international arena.

> I really like the dream —
> how we can make the
> best quality products.

Invigorated is how I'd describe Tony Lo, the morning we met. He arrived at the factory in Taichung after cycling 35 kilometres from his home — a twice-a-week routine, to and fro. This is a man who lives, works, plays, and breathes cycling. No prizes for guessing why he didn't look anywhere near his 67 years.

I tried to wheedle my way to finding out what share he has in this company that he helped build in the last 43 years and he waved it aside, saying, "Very small. That is not important."

What he did talk about, with much respect and admiration throughout the interview, was the man who started the company. In fact, so close is their relationship, despite the 15-year age gap, that they had both agreed to retire together — which they did, a few months after my interview with Lo in 2016.

Lo had played no small role in building this enterprise through the years. When Liu recruited him, he was working with a trading company and was dissatisfied with the quality of products coming out of Taiwan. After meeting Liu, Lo bought into the founder's vision.

"I really like the dream — how we can make the best quality products. Besides, I was young at that time. So, I gave up my job and joined his company," Lo said.

The early years were unsurprisingly challenging. "To be honest, the first couple of years, we hardly got our salaries. It was very tough at the beginning," recalled Lo.

But, in 1977, breakthrough came when Lo sealed the deal with one of the biggest bicycle manufacturers at the time. American bike maker Schwinn decided to take advantage of Taiwan's cost competitiveness by building some of its bicycles there. According to Lo, the clincher for the deal was his company's proprietary material that made frames lighter and stronger.

"At that time, most of the bicycles were made with a high percentage of steel. Steel is strong, but heavy. So, King and I identified the material called chromoly, which is much lighter and stronger than steel. But it's very difficult to manufacture," revealed Lo. The production process was tedious and painstaking, with the frames being hand-made. But with the use of the right technology, Lo's team was able to shorten the process and mass-produce it, with quality intact.

> We wanted to control our own destiny and we wanted to make the best products and meet with the final consumer.

It was a breakthrough that led the management team through a period of relative ease and well-lined pockets. But all good things must come to an end, and that end came when Schwinn decided to move part of their manufacturing to Shenzhen in the 1980s, after acquiring a company there.

It was a needful wake-up call. Liu and Lo, like most manufacturers in Taiwan, had put most of their eggs in the original equipment manufacturer (OEM) basket. In fact, 75% of their business came from making products for other brands.

"We learnt that OEM is not a long-term future and we wanted to control our own destiny and we wanted to make the best products and meet with the final consumer. So we said, 'Okay, we're doing pretty good in the Taiwan market. So, why not take this global?'"

The Giant brand was born in 1981.

Riding the globe

With the know-how they had gathered by making some of the best bicycles in the world, Lo saw a ready market in the Netherlands — a country with a dominant cycling culture and where bicycles outnumber residents.

"We decided to go to Europe first, because bicycles have 240 years of history, starting from Europe. And we said, 'Hey! We make bicycles for the United States, for the best company, Schwinn!'" recalled Lo.

But, his enthusiasm was quickly dampened by the lukewarm response. "They said 'No, this is just medium quality and far from good quality.' Each country had their own local manufacturers. There was no need for other brands. So, it became very, very difficult," Lo confessed. It didn't help that Made-In-Taiwan products were also perceived with a fair amount of scepticism by the Europeans.

But Lo was undeterred. He realised that the only way to make inroads into Europe was to build bikes of exceptional quality. Very simply put, they just had "to make the best bicycle in the world." Back to the drawing board.

A few years later in 1987, they emerged with yet another engineering breakthrough. Giant introduced the world's first bicycle made of carbon fibre composite. Until then, carbon fibre was mainly used in airplanes because of its light weight and strength. The team worked on it for three years and soon could mass-produce it, making carbon-fibre road bikes affordable for the masses.

By then, a sales office was set up in the Netherlands and, ten years later, in 1996, its first and only production plant in Europe was established to reach the market there faster.

The big break for Giant to step into the big league came in 1997, with an offer they couldn't refuse — from the Mecca of the cycling world.

"After we had the carbon fibre bicycles, the Tour de France asked us to provide our bicycles to them, and we were surprised. They knew we had the best bicycles and asked if we were willing to sponsor them and we said, 'Of course!'"

Not only was Giant competing with the best of them, champions also emerged from its team. "That got us attention... it started becoming easier," Lo said.

The company has since sponsored procycling teams that have consistently won various competitions. Lo wouldn't reveal the sponsorship budget although he did say 8% of the company's operating budget is allocated to marketing activities. Estimates put Giant's sponsorship of its Tour de France team, Team Sunweb, at US$15 million.[1] The company has 3 other global teams that it supports. Lo, being a marketing man, firmly believes that this strategy has paid off for the company.

"Working with Tour de France top athletes, we can develop the best bicycles — stronger, lighter. Taking it from there, we built our reputation," he said. Europe has become the company's largest contributor. In 2016, 31% of sales were derived from there, followed closely by 21% from North America and 18% from China.

In a lot of countries, people think we're a local brand. Japan thinks we're Japanese and France thinks we're French!

Giant has been deliberate in establishing a strong presence in the West with nine of its 14 sales offices located in Europe and North America and managed by local employees. "We don't just go there to do it ourselves. We try to find the best people and support them to become very successful. And most people have stayed with us for 20–30 years and their job is to help the local retailers to provide better service to the consumers," said Lo.

The strategy has integrated the brand seamlessly in the various territories. "In a lot of countries, people think we're a local brand. Japan thinks we're Japanese and France thinks we're French! But that's fine. We spend a lot of effort to make the roots very deep," added Lo, pleased with the mistaken identities.

Whether real or apparent, the Made-In-Taiwan label is still plagued with negative perceptions in the West, a point acknowledged by Lo. If not for Giant's innovative product and brand development over the last three decades, it, too, would've fallen prey to the stereotype.

Team Taiwan

As early as 2002, Lo saw the need to develop Taiwan into a bicycle manufacturing hub that could distinguish itself from China, and, indeed, the rest of the world. For one, China was eating its lunch with its prolific production of entry-level bicycles. Lo realised they could not compete with the Chinese in quantity or price. The only way forward was to build *better* bicycles through quality and innovation.

> Just like in Germany, they make BMW and Mercedes Benz. So, why can't Taiwan make top quality bicycles?

He believed that, to stand out from the rest of the competition, bicycle manufacturers in the country had to work as a bloc to implement the best practices and share ideas. For Lo, there were no limits to his vision. "Just like in Germany, they make BMW and Mercedes Benz. So, why can't Taiwan make top quality bicycles?" Lo asked, rhetorically.

In 2003, Lo gathered a group of 13 local manufacturers to share ideas and improve the quality of bicycles from Taiwan. Today, under the moniker A-Team, a group of 20 bicycle makers continue to work together to raise the profile of Taiwan as the home of high quality and affordable bicycles.

Their efforts were rewarded when Taiwan became the first country in Asia to host a premiere cycling event, the Velo-city conference, in

2016. Since 1980, this gathering of the European Cyclists' Federation had been held throughout Europe and North America. Winning the bid to host it was a coup for the Taiwanese. Not only did the international cycling community recognise the country as a centre of innovative manufacturing solutions, but it was also a nod towards the country's efforts to promote cycling as a lifestyle through its infrastructure and administration.

Creating a cycling culture

Giant Bicycles grew from a struggling company of 35 employees in the 70s to the global giant it is today, with a staff of 11,000 worldwide and the title of top revenue earner. Beyond just building a successful business, however, Lo and founder Liu have created a cycling lifestyle that has complemented Taiwan's reputation as a bicycle manufacturing hub.

In Taipei, ubiquitous bright orange rental bicycles zip past one another on bicycle lanes criss-crossing the city. The bike sharing service, YouBike, is designed and operated by Giant. Present in five other cities in Taiwan, YouBike has become part of the city landscape. The programme was launched in 2009 and allows cyclists to pick up a bike from one station and return it to a secured rack in another location. In Taipei City alone, there're almost 200 YouBike stations. According to Lo, each bicycle is used at least eight times a day. To date, 66 million rides have been recorded in Taipei.

The surge of interest in cycling started in 2007 when, at the age of 73, Giant founder King Liu went on a tour of Taiwan on a bicycle. The media was abuzz as cameras followed Liu throughout the 15-day tour, over 575 miles. The gauntlet was thrown down by the septuagenarian. "People began to say, 'If that old guy can do it, then maybe we can do that,'" Lo recalled.

The company began organising cycling tours, initially, among industry players. Since then, Lo reported, there are at least 1000 groups doing tours in Taiwan.

In fact, being the consummate marketing man and given to hyperbole, Lo went as far as to assert, "If you are Taiwanese, you must do cycling around Taiwan once at least. Otherwise, you are not a Taiwanese." When we met, Lo was preparing for his ninth tour of Taiwan.

On a mission

Entrepreneurs often tout passion before profits. I heard it again from Lo. Profit, he said, was a by-product. "If you do all the other things right, the profit will come," he said assuredly. And it's hard not to believe him. Not only did he build up a global brand over 35 years and a company that's the top earner in its class by revenue, Lo went beyond the dollars and cents to the creation of a culture that a few in their lifetime could claim credit for.

"We never really wanted to become big and we never wanted to become number one. But we wanted to do a good job; we wanted to become the only one in manufacturing, R&D, in many things. So, we just kept trying to do things right," Lo said.

> If you are not riding a bicycle yet, I've got to save you!

Far from being an overnight success, the story of Giant's foray to the West is an example of dogged determination, innovative use of technology, and, above all, an abiding belief in a dream to build high-quality bicycles, and beyond that, to create a lifestyle.

Lo is given to superlatives when he gets excited. He says he has "the best bicycles" and "the best system in the world." By most accounts, they aren't empty boasts. He speaks with missionary zeal about cycling as a lifestyle. He calls the 3,500 Giant Bicycles stores around the world "churches," where the altar call to salespeople is to "Go there and tell people (cycling) is so great and help them to enjoy it."

His mandate is clear. "We have a mission to save all people," he declared. Then, on cue, he turned to me and said, "If you are not riding a bicycle yet, I've got to save you!"

Note

1 Stuart Clark, "Which Tour de France team has the largest budget?", Cycling Weekly, 19 July 2016.

Chapter 9

The Mettle to Take on the World

Kumar Mangalam Birla
Aditya Birla Group

H e had big shoes to fill, with three generations of pre-eminent industrialists before him. The first was his great-grandfather, who was a close associate of Mahatma Gandhi, followed by his father who was named "India's first global industrialist," with a commemorative stamp bearing his image.

Kumar Mangalam Birla had the weight of a country's expectations on his shoulders. And it wasn't as if he could take his time to learn the ropes. At the age of 28, his father had passed away suddenly from cancer and young Birla was hurled to the top post of a regional conglomerate that raked in a turnover of US$1.6 billion in 1995, the year he took over.

Sceptics, naturally, abounded. But he silenced them by growing the Aditya Birla Group not just within Asia, where his father had already made strides, but globally. Today, the Group with a turnover of over US$40 billion has businesses spanning 15 sectors, from commodities to chemicals and metals to textiles, in 36 countries.

The global conglomerate traces its roots to the 19th century with the early Birlas' foray into the cotton business. It was Kumar Birla's great-grandfather, Ghanshyam Das Birla (or GD Birla), who thrust the family into the league of industrialists by starting businesses in textiles, cement, aluminium, and chemicals. In fact, the iconic Indian automobile, the Ambassador, was built by this fabled family. GD Birla was also involved in the fight for freedom along with Gandhi. Freedom fighters would meet in the Birla home to discuss their mission to free India from the British Raj.

When Kumar Birla took over the company he was only beginning to find his place in the world that his father, a giant in the Indian business community, had suddenly left vacant. He was, in his own words, "an unknown quantity."

But it was in the darkest of moments that true allegiances arose. "My family was very strongly behind me in this, stood behind me like a rock. And I would think that the entire organisation, almost without exception, stood behind me like a rock," Birla recalled. "They had a great sense of loyalty, emotional connect with the family, with my father. And they all rallied around. It was quite amazing and very, very touching."

Reaching further

I watched Birla at work when he chaired a press conference in 2013 to announce the acquisition of two cement plants in Gujarat. In the face of a highly vocal and circumspect Indian media, he was calm, authoritative, and knowledgeable. Other older members in the panel deferred to the then 46-year-old. A local journalist once likened Birla's equanimity to that of the Hindu god, Shiva. It's an apt imagery for a man whose impassive facial expressions belie a steely determination and audacious ambitions.

Superlatives such as *largest, biggest, best, leading, top*, and *No. 1* are often used to describe the Group's businesses, and the achievements are not fortuitous. Birla would have you know, unequivocally, that if they're not top three, "then we question why we are in the business in the first place," he said.

It was with this dauntless posturing that Birla set a target in 2008 of US$65 billion in Group revenue by 2016. As with all ambitious goals, some you attain, some you don't. The company fell 40% short. Even when we met in 2013, the goal was already elusive and Birla conceded that the changes in the Indian economy and the depreciation of the US dollar against the rupee threw the spanner in the works for the company. "I think that it's a very audacious target. But at the same time, it's very well thought through," he insisted. Almost grudgingly, he conceded, "While I still see us achieving the target, I think that we could be delayed by a year or two, because of the external environment."

Today, more than half the Group's turnover comes from its overseas ventures, a move that began with Birla's father. When Kumar Birla took over, the company had already acquired the title of one of India's first multinationals. It had a strong presence in Southeast Asia and even in Egypt, with manufacturing plants and mining projects.

However, Birla stretched the company's reach to the West, with a shopping spree rarely seen in India then. Starting in 1998, the Group acquired two pulp mills in Canada and later formed a joint venture with Canada-based Sun Life Insurance in 2000. In 2011, the company paid US$875 million for Atlanta-based Colombian Chemical to catapult the Group to the position of the largest producer of carbon black, a material commonly used in tyres. In the same year, the Swedish producer of cellulose for fabric production Domsjo Fabriker was also purchased for US$360 million.

Looking beyond the sensationalism of Birla's shopping spree in the West are valuable lessons in mergers and acquisitions. While 50% of M&As fail in their business and financial objectives,[1] the Aditya Birla Group's acquisitions have been successful both in expanding its markets and achieving its long-term vision for the merged entities.

For Birla, this is the result of painstaking deliberation and calculations. "A lot of time is spent thinking through why, what value would it add, how long would it take to add the kind of value we're expecting. Pitfalls, possible negatives, possible upsides. So, a lot of work that goes into that and we wouldn't get into a process of merger or acquisition without having thought through all of these very well."

The one acquisition that stands out for Birla is the Group's costliest by far. In 2007, its subsidiary, Hindalco, struck a deal to purchase Atlanta-based Novelis, the world's largest producer of aluminium sheets. The price tag — US$6 billion. Another part of the bid that raised eyebrows was the unusual fact that the acquirer was four times smaller in sales than the acquired.[2]

"That was a quantum leap... I think that one really got us thinking," conceded Birla.

Before Novelis came along, Hindalco was focused on producing the raw materials for aluminium. While it was profitable, it was also subjected to price fluctuations. The downstream business was not as volatile and it was, happily, Novelis' forte. The company had a presence in 11 countries with 12,500 employees and blue chip customers like Coca Cola, Ford and Tetrapak, for whom they produced value-added products like rolled aluminium for specific uses.

Of course, the fact that Novelis was a market leader sat very well with the team in India. There was also "the quality of people, the quality of plant machinery, of the product, and the kind of R&D that they have. So, that was more asset-specific, and we were looking for an asset in that space. It seemed to fit in perfectly," Birla pointed out. Merging the technology and innovation of a global leader with the low cost and high demand in India was a recipe for success. Projects were created in India to expand Novelis' market while the exchange of knowledge and opportunities grew the fortunes of the new entity.

However, look beneath the hood and the picture was not always this rosy. It was a rocky start for the Hindalco-Novelis merger with the onslaught of the Global Financial Crisis that hit a year after the acquisition. Internally, Novelis had earlier signed off on some loss-making contracts that dragged down the performance of the company. The day after the deal was announced Hindalco's scrip price fell by 13% and its market capitalisation plunged by US$600 million.[3] Shareholders were not happy with Hindalco taking on Novelis' US$2.4 billion debt.

But the patience and belief in what they were doing were rewarded. The managing director of Hindalco, remarked that it would've taken ten years to build its own assets to what Novelis already had. The gamble paid off in 2010–2011, when Hindalco registered its largest jump in revenue to more than US$5 billion. That's more than a two-fold increase compared to the same period before the acquisition of Novelis. Added to that, the transfer of skills in the downstream business bolstered Hindalco's expertise — the attention to quality and service, product development and brand building were areas that boosted the skill set of the Indian company.

The benefits were mutual. Before the acquisition, Novelis was running a loss of US$275 million in 2006. Four years later, in 2010, it got out of the red to register a very respectable US$400 million in net earnings. It's grown steadily since, with a topline of US$10 billion and operating profit of US$1 billion in 2017. In all, the acquisition catapulted Hindalco to the top of the table of rolled aluminium producers globally. Additionally, it extended Hindalco's reach right across the supply chain of the aluminium business.

The perennial debate between organic growth and acquisitions prevails in any discussion on growth. The debt chalked up for acquisitions can, of course, be substantial. In Aditya Birla's case financing costs were pushing north of US$260 million in 2014/2015.[4] But Birla justified his close to 20 acquisitions by citing the company's overall strategy. Acquisitions, he said, were to give them new markets, technologies, capital sourcing of raw materials. "The idea has been to bolster the business and create more solid businesses," Birla asserted.

Processes and people

Theories abound on reasons for the failure of the M&A deals. A lack of discipline in planning, incompatible systems and processes, overestimating market sentiment and the inability to react quickly to the changing business environment are some of the factors. In a study of Hindalco's acquisition of Novelis, Nirmalya Kumar, a former senior executive of Tata Sons and an academic at the Singapore Management University, puts its success down to concerted efforts to align the two companies' systems in the area of financial reporting, business processes, market distribution and organisational planning.[5]

I think that a lot of it, at the end of the day, is about building confidence in the people, in the entity that you're taking over, and plugging into their hearts and minds.

And it is in the area of management and people planning that the head honcho of the Group chose to focus on when asked what made their acquisitions work. Birla was aware that, while "processes and systems are institutionalised and are not ad-hoc," provisions must also be made to "encourage the entrepreneurial spirit of our people."

In the final analysis, the post-acquisition strategy must be about people. "I think that a lot of it, at the end of the day, is about building confidence in the people, in the entity that you're taking over, and plugging into their hearts and minds. It's just not about balance sheets coming together," he said.

"We've normally retained the teams in the companies that we've taken over as a principle. And it's about motivating them. It's about making them feel one with the Group. It's about sharing the dream with them. And it's amazing how well that can work with human endeavour and the quality of endeavours that people would want to put in and be willing to put in as long as they know there is genuineness in that intent," said Birla.

As the largest Indian company in the US, Hindalco proudly points out that 95% of its employees are Americans. And out of the 19 senior management personnel in the US outfit, only two are from the Indian parent company. Steve Fisher, the president and CEO, retained his post after acquisition. The practice of running Novelis as an independent entity has proven to be a winning strategy for the organisation.

Taking the experience home

Fifteen years after the Aditya Birla Group made its first foray to the West, India has come to an uptick in its economic cycle. The country's GDP since 2013 has been ranging from 6–8% and this trend is expected to continue until 2020.[6] The various economic reforms initiated by the Modi government has also given businesses much to cheer about.

Even the much-cited World Bank's Ease of Doing Business report, which had traditionally given India a low rating, sent India's ranking soaring 30 places in its 2018 report, placing it in the top 100 for the first time.[7] All these are a positive confluence of events that have justified Birla's shift in focus since 2014.

> Being in markets where we're up against the best-in-class competition, it's something that we're very used to.

Soon after the Modi government was installed, Birla was reported saying, "In the next five years, when we make an investment decision, as opposed to not looking at India, India will be a preferred destination."[8] True to his word, growth in the company has been centred on businesses at home.

And the Group is well-placed to ride the developments in its home country with the breadth of experience and expertise garnered from its overseas ventures. Not only has its returns on offshore investments allowed the Group to make massive investments in India in multiple sectors but, being a global multinational, it has the added advantage of exposure to best practices in the 36 countries it operates in. Foreign competition in their home turf is par for the course, now that the country has loosened its hold on foreign participation in its economy since June 2016.

"We work in markets where you have the toughest competitors globally. Being in markets where we're up against the best-in-class competition, it's something that we're very used to. And we actually enjoy that because it brings out the best in us. And I think foreign investors coming into India is something that's happening. It's bound to happen more and we welcome that," Birla had said back in 2013, even before reforms on foreign investment.

Conversely, with uncertainty in global markets today, protectionism in the US and European volatility following Brexit, the Aditya Birla Group is less bullish about its acquisitions overseas. If anything, the sale of Indian conglomerate Tata's stake in UK-based Corus in 2016, nine years after Tata bought it for a record US$12 billion (the largest foreign investment by an Indian company), could be a bellwether for Indian expansion overseas in this season.

For Kumar Mangalam Birla and the Aditya Birla Group, the push and pull factors through time has seen the company spreading its wings to the West only to come home to roost in this high season of India's growth — bigger, better, and stronger.

Notes

1 Nirmalya Kumar, "How Emerging Giants are Rewriting the Rules of M&A", Harvard Business Review, May 2009.

2. "Hindalco to acquire Novelis for $6 bn", Livemint, 12 Feb 2007, <http://www.livemint.com/Home-Page/v8Nz0EASvQJUD7vYrLG9WL/Hindalco-to-acquire-Novelis-for-6-bn.html>

3 Nirmalya Kumar, "How Emerging Giants are Rewriting the Rules of M&A", Harvard Business Review, May 2009.

4. Hindalco Industries Limited, Annual Report 2014/2015.

5 Nirmalya Kumar, May 2009.

6 Akshay Shah, "India's Economy Surpasses That of Great Britain", 16 December 2016, Forbes.

7 "India Jumps Doing Business Rankings with Sustained Reform Focus", World Bank Press Release, 31 October 2017, <http://www.worldbank.org/en/news/press-release/2017/10/31/india-jumps-doing-business-rankings-with-sustained-reform-focus>

8 "Billionaire Who Shunned India Does U-Turn on Modi Overhaul", Bloomberg, 12 November 2014.

Part IV

GROWING LOCAL BRANDS

Not too far in the distant past, any product made in the US or Europe was invariably seen as superior. Save for products from Japan, it was common even for Asians to turn up their noses at brands from their region.

With rising protectionism restricting foreign players in local markets, the transfer of technology boosting the quality of local products, and the inroads into distribution networks giving homegrown brands greater presence, local names in large countries such as Indonesia and India have taken the lead in consumer preferences over their foreign competitors. This is particularly true in the case of the food and beverage business.

In some cases, price has a big part to play in the equation. In Indonesia, bread, for instance, used to be a luxury afforded to the small middle class. However, with growing income levels, affordability, and changing lifestyles, bread has grown in popularity. And the entrance of a local player at the right time and at the right price has played no small role in that trajectory.

Interestingly, in the beverage market in India, price differences between international and local brands are negligible and, in some instances, non-existent. Over the years, multinational brands have acquired local bottling facilities and distributors and kept costs down. Yet, local brands have pipped the global giants in their own game.

The companies highlighted in this section are early entrants in the food and beverage business on their home turf. They've taken on multinational giants and proven to be players to be reckoned with. The women who helm the companies show how they keep their brands the leaders of the pack in very crowded and challenging markets.

Chapter 10

Refreshing India

Schauna Chauhan
Parle Agro, India

Walk into any major supermarket in any big Indian city and you'll see a panoply of brands in the drinks aisle. Many of the brands are local heroes that cater to Indians, either by taste or by price. Talk to any analyst in the fast-moving consumer goods industry in the country, however, and they'll name you three beverage brands, in particular, that dominate: Coca Cola, PepsiCo, and Parle Agro. The first two are, of course, the usual suspects, while the third is an Indian staple that's been in the market since 1959. The carbonated drink that the company's founder developed with his brother in the 1970s continues to compete for the top spot, with the two global giants' signature drinks.

Thums Up is an iconic carbonated drink, well-loved by Indians. It was opportunistically introduced in 1977, the year Coca Cola was expelled by the nationalist government. Restrictive conditions were imposed on foreign companies that forced many to exit the country. At that time, Coca Cola was the best-selling carbonated drink and had been in India for 10 years. But unhappiness over the company's earnings at the expense of local bottlers (reports say return on capital was a staggering 800% – 1200%)[1] compelled the government to place two unacceptable conditions before the American company: reveal the secret formula of its signature drink and give up the majority ownership of the company. Those conditions could only lead to one course of action. Coca Cola took the high road and left India.

Parle, the company behind Thums Up, wasted no time in filling the gap and very quickly launched itself to a dominant market position, with 80% share. The company was then owned by two brothers, Ramesh and Prakash Chauhan.

The company enjoyed its heyday with the protection of the Indian government until the latter took an about-turn in its policy and liberalised the economy, inviting foreign companies back to the country to boost its share of foreign investments. Coca Cola wasted no time in re-entering the Indian market in 1993, after a 16-year hiatus. They did what most international outfits with deep pockets would do — they acquired companies who were leaders in the soft drink market. That meant having an established distribution network, bottling facilities and brands. One company they looked to was Parle.

With a deal the Chauhan brothers could not turn down, Parle, along with its best sellers Thums Up, Limca, and Maaza, was sold to Coca Cola for US$60 million. Today, the three brands continue to count themselves among the top sellers in India, a country of 1.2 billion people.

The sale of Parle by the two brothers was a painful decision. In his biography, Ramesh Chauhan related how Coca Cola had persuaded most of Parle's bottlers to partner with them, leaving the brothers little choice but to sell or be trounced by the giant. In various accounts, Ramesh was said to be in tears when he signed the agreement.[2]

Part of the contract that the brothers signed was a non-competition clause that prohibited them from selling any carbonated drink for the next 10 years. After the sale of Parle, Ramesh branched out to create the best-selling bottled water, Bisleri, under his company Parle Bisleri, while Prakash held on to the two remaining bottling units of Parle in Mumbai and continued its beverage business under the name, Parle Agro.

Coca Cola, in the meantime, didn't reinvent the wheel when they took over Thums Up, Limca, and Maaza. After all, the three top sellers under Parle had already worked their way to the taste buds of Indians.

What is of interest is how the newly-formed Parle Agro would negotiate its way back to the good old days of market dominance, not with colas, since the brothers had signed out of that option, but with a lucrative and uniquely Indian fruit drink. The beverage captured the richness of a special species of fruit that originated in India: the Alphonso mango.

The second-generation entrepreneurs

Today, Parle Agro is run by Prakash's two daughters. When I met Schauna Chauhan, joint managing director of the company, in 2012 in Mumbai, she was a fresh-faced 35-year-old. Her younger sister Nadia was the marketing genius behind the brand, while Schauna oversaw the operations. Father Prakash had retired by then but was still overseeing big decisions.

Schauna Chauhan carried a confidence beyond her age, having been in the business for the past 14 years. Yet, she would also demonstrate a disarming unguardedness, bursting into a girlish giggle every now and then. She made no apologies for her style of micromanagement and yet would ask candidly at junctures of the interview how she should answer sensitive questions. Her vulnerability seemed incongruent with her position as the co-head of a food and beverage behemoth, but it was also refreshingly sincere. Here was a young successor ready to learn, invigorated and primed to take on the challenges ahead.

Today, Parle Agro products are found in 44 countries raking in a topline of US$615 million in 2017.[3] While beverages constitute the company's top vertical, other products that contribute to its coffers are water, confectionary, and PET bottles. But the star of the show is its very own mango drink.

Created in 1985, Frooti jostles for the top three spots among its competitors, Maaza (a former Parle product, now owned by Coca Cola) and Slice (a brand under PepsiCo). Parle Agro claims Frooti has a market share of 28% in the mango drink segment, and the Chauhan sisters aren't letting up on their goal to take it to the number one spot. In 2015, Frooti was relaunched with a new look and a new campaign, featuring Bollywood A-lister Shah Rukh Khan as its ambassador, all for the whopping sum of US$15 million. Not resting on its laurels,

Frooti branched out into the carbonated category with Frooti Fizz in 2017.

The ability of local brands to run with the horses of international players is unique in each country. The study of Parle Agro's Frooti shows what it takes to play with the big boys.

The Bollywood factor

The jury is out on which of the top three brands of mango drink tastes better. It's the perennial Coke–Pepsi taste test, except this one now includes a third protagonist. Margins for mango drinks are thinner than that of their carbonated counterparts. So, keeping costs low is crucial. Pricing the product is key and all three competitors have kept their prices comparable with a INR5 (US$0.08) difference among them. It's also hard to distinguish which marketing campaign has boosted the fortunes of the brands since all have opted to go the way of Bollywood endorsers. It's a hugely popular marketing strategy in India for companies with deep pockets.

The godfather of Bollywood, Amitabh Bachchan, for instance, is as popular an actor as he is a spokesman for countless brands in India, from pens and batteries to cars and banks. PepsiCo has been using Katrina Kaif for Slice since 2008. Not to be outdone, Coca Cola doubled its star power for Maaza with Imran Khan and Parineeti Chopra, before opting for another duo, Varun Dhawan and Gulshan Grover, in 2015.

> Getting (Shah Rukh Khan) to be the ambassador for Frooti would just help us in terms of growing the market further.

Although late in the game, Parle Agro pulled no punches with the king of endorsers, Shah Rukh Khan, in its 2013 campaign. "Getting (Khan) to be the ambassador for Frooti would just help us in terms of growing the market further, getting into different cross-sections of the market," explained Chauhan.

While Frooti has traditionally been known as a kids' drink, Parle Agro hopes to expand the profile to include youths and families. And having a wildly popular star like Shah Rukh Khan speak for them would certainly not hurt.

"Celebrities are looked at as cool, as glamorous, and that is what the brand requires today," said Chauhan. "Kids can relate to stars, they see them as glamorous. A lot of people are star struck. Bollywood is very huge here. So, we're hoping that this would have the double-digit growth it would bring." Chauhan should know all about star power since she married a Bollywood actor, Bikram Saluja, in 2004.

In 2015, Frooti did indeed see a growth of 12%–15%, but it's hard to tell if it's the result of the draw of Shah Rukh Khan or simply, as sister Nadia acknowledged in another interview, the growth of the market for mango drinks; it's so huge that even a 1% increase in the consumption of the drink would have favourable knock-on effects on brands.[4] Estimates in 2017 put the size of the mango drink market in India at about US$800 million, with a growth rate of 8%.[5]

While the jury is still out on the returns on lavish campaigns featuring Bollywood endorsers, Parle Agro seems convinced this is the way to stay ahead of the competition. They've recently signed on another big name, Priyanka Chopra, for their other best-selling drink: Appy Fizz. The carbonated apple drink packaged in a sophisticated long-necked bottle with black accents has had no competition since it was launched in 2005. The company invested US$10 million in that campaign.

Reaching the rural folks

If there is one piece of quantitative data that can lend some perspective on the mango drink war among competing brands, it's in the distribution network of various players. India has the seventh largest land mass in the world, and almost 70% of the billion-plus population live in rural areas and make up 30–50% of the market for basic consumer goods. So, ignoring this segment of the market is not an option for major fast-moving consumer goods players.

"You see, India's like a pyramid," Chauhan explained. "You have very small niche market at the top, which can actually afford these high-end luxury items. Then you have the middle class and then you have this huge number of people in the lower class. So, the rural market is very important."

To reach the rural areas and to reach them fast enough, manufacturing facilities need to be located strategically across the subcontinent. Coca Cola has about 30 bottling plants manufacturing Maaza,[6] distributing to more than 1.5 million outlets.[7] With a similar number of plants producing Slice, PepsiCo has about 1 million outlets stocking their mango drink while Parle Agro has 1.3 million outlets, served by the lowest number of factories — 14.[8]

Intermediaries or channels play a crucial role in getting products from the factory to the consumer. Parle Agro relies on 4,000 channel partners to market, distribute, and sell its products. "Distribution is the most important because how else do you go? You have to figure out how to reach those rural markets where the infrastructure is not available," said Chauhan.

> You have to figure out how to reach those rural markets where the infrastructure is not available.

With poor infrastructure, getting the drinks to the consumers is a challenge. Throw in the short shelf life of fruit drinks, and you have a conundrum. Frooti is best consumed within 14 days after it leaves the factory. Vendors have complained of receiving drinks that are close to their sell-by date. To overcome this problem, Parle Agro has set itself the goal of adding one manufacturing location every year to its production capacity to ensure the shortest possible time from factory to store.

Its eye on the goal is unwavering. "We're very conservative, but yet very aggressive. We are a sales-driven organisation. We don't believe in losing even one consumer. So, for us to ensure that we're able to cater to each and every consumer of ours, to ensure that we're able to get into the sales demand, we focus a lot on the infrastructure," said Chauhan.

The location of each plant is determined by the market they want to enter and, then, by the availability of utilities, such as power and water. In a country where power shortages are common, these considerations can't be taken lightly. Coincidentally, or not, at the time we met, Chauhan was scheduled to visit a new plant in Varanasi, Uttar Pradesh, to iron out problems there. The factory was supposed to have begun operations two months earlier, if not for the lack of electricity.

Water supply is also patchy in the country. In 2016, Coca Cola shuttered three plants in remote parts of India citing the lack of demand there. Activists, however, hailed the closure of the factory in Jaipur, in particular, as a victory for them. They had been campaigning for a decade for it to be shut down, alleging that the plant was depleting groundwater in the area and affecting the livelihood of farmers in the region.

Apart from utilities, other amenities such as schools and medical centres have to be available for employees and their families at the plant. Infrastructure development, or the lack of it, remains a drag on companies seeking to expand their footprint across the country.

One drink, many forms

To keep itself one step ahead of the competition, Parle Agro offers Frooti in 11 different packaging for different segments of the market. The drink is presented in returnable glass bottles (RGBs) for hotels, cafés and restaurants, six differently-sized PET bottles, and four sizes in Tetra Paks. In fact, Frooti was the first mango drink in Tetra Pak when it was introduced in 1985. It's made good use of this format as it has claimed the lead position in the Tetra Pak segment of the mango drink market.

"You want to be available in different packaging to offer to different consumers," explained Chauhan on the need for cross-sectional marketing. "Some people like to drink in Tetra Pak — you can carry the Tetra Pack in your tiffin bag, in your tiffin box, and take it to school. On airlines, you see the Frooti packs on your tray, which can fit properly. When you go to college you will drink in, maybe, bottles. It's much cooler, much more fun… The small shops, they seem to be selling a lot more glass bottles and consumers find it much cooler to drink from a glass bottle. So, it's just to make it convenient for the different types of consumers that you are catering to."

> Consumers find it much cooler to drink from a glass bottle.

Data mined from the sales team had revealed that outlets that used to sell only 600-mililitre PET bottles of Frooti sold more 250 millilitre Tetra Paks when they began to stock it. The challenge for the team is to cater to different segments with their different packaging mix.

The decision on how much to put in a pack is intuitive, relying on standard sizes in the market. But the ideas can also be serendipitous.

Parle Agro was the first company to launch a drink in a 90-mililitre triangular Tetra Pak in 2004, making it an all-time favourite of school-going children who can pack the drink neatly with their lunches.

The mini packs are founder Prakash Chauhan's brainchild and it came about one day while the patriarch was sitting in Mumbai's infamous traffic.

"He was at a signal light, and he wanted to eat," Chauhan related of her father's *aha* moment. "You get these people that come on the streets to sell you these *chana sing*, it's like a quick snack that you have. And so he picked up one of those, and he said, 'Now I need a drink.' And that's when he thought that maybe the 200 ml pack is too big a size for something that you want just a sip of. So why not look at a 90 ml pack!"

The triangular packet became an instant success not only because of its nifty packaging, but at INR2.50 (about US$0.05) when it was launched, children could well afford it too. A new market opened up overnight. In fact, it was perhaps this differentiation that branded Frooti as a kids' drink, an image that the company is now trying to shed by targeting the 15–30 age group, with its Bollywood campaign.

Getting over lemons

Operating in an environment as unpredictable as India means that players must be nimble and quick to change course. Resources, in the case of Parle Agro, must also be optimally utilized, particularly when they are so thinly spread by the range of products and the variations within each. Tough decisions must be made when new products don't sell well. When do you give it more time to justify the initial investment in product development and when do you pull the plug to stop the bleeding?

While determination is a common mark of entrepreneurs, stubbornness can be their downfall. Refusing to recognise the signs to cut losses is an all too common story of companies left along the wayside. Parle Agro has had its fair share of failures. Lemons that they've had to drop when the market just didn't bite.

"Lemon didn't work," declared Chauhan when our conversation turned to the failure of LMN, a lemon drink that the company launched in 2009. "I think because (Indian) families preferred to make *nimbu pani*.

Nimbu pani is a drink that every household makes at home. And I think people or families just found it better to make their own *nimbu pani* than have a lemon drink in a package. So, we stopped it after 2 years." That said, PepsiCo and Coca Cola both launched their lemon drinks at about the same time as LMN and still produce them today.

Another failure which the company was quick to kill was Saint, the company's first 100% juice drink. It had hoped to capitalise on the growing demand for healthy drinks. In 2008, Saint hit the shelves in one-litre bottles at INR100, or US$2.50 at that time. According to Chauhan, the price was the cause of its downfall. Within two years, it was taken off the market as lowering the price was not an option. "Our margins would have been lowered. So, it doesn't make any sense to be manufacturing a drink that is not profitable for long," she said, matter-of-factly.

> I think it's important to take these decisions to know when to put an end to something...

"I think it's important to take these decisions to know when to put an end to something because you could be continually selling more, but because of your negative margin, your bottom line is getting hit. At the end, what are you actually achieving? Nothing. So, it's important to keep a good eye on that and to be able to take the decision at the right time."

By far, the costliest mistake for the company has been the decision to shut down an entire manufacturing plant when the product it produced flopped. In 2006, Parle Agro made its confectionary debut with a chewy tamarind sweet, Simply Imlee. It had hoped to ride on its wide distribution network. However, that product failed, and the decision was made to write-off the factory.

Chauhan was almost philosophical about the lessons learnt. "I think there are certain things that you just don't know what's going to happen. But unless you take that risk, and unless you have the courage to do something about what you have in mind, you're never going to know the outcome. So, if you believe in something, and if there's something that you want to do, you have to get up and do it; don't just sit and talk about it."

Perhaps being a privately-held family business makes mistakes more forgivable and the organisation more nimble: decisions get made faster, both to develop a new product as well as to end one.

Not that there've been a lack of suitors along the way. In 2010, Japan-based Asahi Breweries sought to partner with Parle Agro but their offer was turned down. "We're a family-held company, and we plan to be a family-held company," declared Chauhan.

The proof of the pudding is in the bottom line. With a compound annual growth rate of about 11% since 2002, the hits have obviously far outnumbered the misses, and the company's ability to stay agile keeps it primed to push the envelope constantly.

***

It is admirable that a company much smaller than the multinationals that it competes with has been able to hold its place in the mango drink market for as long as it has. The combination of marketing, distribution, packaging, and the discipline to optimize resources has kept Parle Agro's finger on the pulse of consumer tastes in India.

Growth trends bode well for the company as estimates have put the juice drink market in India at US$21 billion by 2018.[9] Consider, too, the preference for healthier alternatives, the burgeoning middle class and the country's path to becoming the most populous country in the world by 2018, and you have a happy confluence of factors, boosting the forecast for Parle Agro.

With these facts, however, competition will only get more intense, for not only are the majors stepping up their efforts to capture the growing market, other local players are increasingly taking up space as well.

For Parle Agro, with its dominance in the market coupled with the spirited posture of the founding family, the near future is certainly something it can drink to. But the dynamism and the unpredictable course of business in India makes resting on laurels a dangerous seat to take.

Notes

1 "Coca-Cola: The hard company behind the soft drink", 15 September 1977, Indiatoday.in, <http://indiatoday.intoday.in/story/coca-cola-the-hard-company-behind-the-soft-drink/1/435711.html>

2   Surajeet Das Gupta, "Ramesh Chauhan was a fighter. I enjoyed that", 21 January 2013, Business Standard, <http://www.business-standard.com/article/beyond-business/-ramesh-chauhan-was-a-fighter-i-enjoyed-that-111111200041_1.html>

3   "Parle Agro looks to expand to south India", Livemint, 11 April 2018, <https://www.livemint.com/Companies/nacUls1IFvdYy1DPWqwcRM/Parle-Agro-looks-to-expand-in-south-India.html>

4   Shilpa Ranipeta, "Parle's Fruit Drinks Adding Fizz to Growth", 2 May 2016, Business Television India, <http://www.btvi.in/article/read/news/5484/parle-s-fruit-drinks-adding-fizz-to-growth>

5   "Parle expands sparkling juices segment with Frooti Fizz", 8 March 2017, moneycontrol.com, <http://www.moneycontrol.com/news/business/companies/parle-expands-sparkling-juices-segmentfrooti-fizz-1057513.html>

6   "Coca Cola targets to make Maaza a $1 bn brand by 2023", Business Standard, 24 June 2016.

7   "Can rebranded Frooti and Slice wash out Maaza?", The Economic Times, 15 April 2015.

8   "Parle Agro looks to expand to south India", Livemint, 11 April 2018.

9   "India's packaged juice market has huge untapped potential", FnBNews.com, 4 March 2016, <http://www.fnbnews.com/Top-News/indias-packaged-juice-market-has-huge-untapped-potential-38596>

Chapter 11

The Rise of Sari Roti

Wendy Yap
Nippon Indosari Corpindo, Indonesia

The discussion of consumption patterns in Indonesia often hinges on the much-touted burgeoning consumer class and the rapid pace of development in the country. Indonesia will be the fifth largest economy in the world by 2030. This middle class will have an average income of US$11,300 per household by then.[1] McKinsey estimates that 50 million people will join this group every year, and 2020 will see 86 million consumers fuelling the economy.[2] Consumption as a percentage of GDP was at 55% in 2016, according to the World Bank, and the number is expected to grow.

While in many parts of the world, consumers would view global brands as aspirational and desirable, Indonesians, by contrast, prefer local brands, perceiving them as more trustworthy and, for pragmatic reasons, value for money, according to McKinsey. However, this trend may change with more disposable income available to the consuming class and as more foreign players enter the market with the liberalisation of the economy, announced by President Joko Widodo in 2016. The measures introduced allow greater equity by foreigners and, in some industries, as much as a 100% of a company.

For local bread maker Nippon Indosari Corpindo, Indonesia's largest bread manufacturer in the mass market segment, these new vagaries should keep the company on its toes. But its pole position, the intricacies of operating in this expansive archipelago, and their unique advantages make for an informative case study of how local brands continue to play a dominant role in this population of 260 million.

Sari Roti is Indosari's flagship brand. Before it hit the shelves 20 years ago, Indonesians had their choice of breads from home and small bakeries, but output was negligible because of the undisputed staple of rice and noodles and the limited disposable income of the population. Over the years, as the founding CEO and owner of Indosari, Wendy Yap, pointed out, it was the evolving lifestyle of Indonesians that boosted the popularity of bread in the country.

"When we first started, there were more people working and not having time to eat breakfast because it takes a longer time to commute. The traffic jams got worse and they wanted something on the run," said Yap. What better option than a handy and affordable loaf or a bun as a filler.

For Indosari's fortuitous beginnings, it's a clichéd but veritable phenomenon of being at the right place at the right time.

Protesters need to eat too

Shortly after Sari Roti made its debut in its home market in 1997, political demonstrations broke out on the streets of Jakarta. Students descended on the city for several weeks denouncing the Suharto regime for its failed policies and corruption, as the financial system crumbled and unemployment and inflation rose. During the Asian Financial Crisis of 1997–1998, things came to a head when the rupiah plunged 400% against the greenback. Resentment against the government that had for a long time been stifled, boiled over.

While it would've been inopportune by most accounts to launch a new product then, the street protests served as a boon to Sari Roti. With the panic sparked by the demonstrations, households began stockpiling food, and since Sari Roti was the only pre-packaged bread with a 5-day shelf life, it was quickly snapped up.

We could not sell enough!

"Our bread was always sold out at the supermarket," recalled Yap. "We could not sell enough! There was just so much demand. Everything was all sold out. So, it was actually a good time for us."

Indosari was the brainchild of Yap's father, Piet Yap, a trusted executive of the late Liem Sioe Liong, also known as Sudono Salim. Salim was one of the right-hand men of former president Suharto. In the 1950s, Yap Sr had made a name for himself as a commodities trader and, in 1968, he set up the largest flour mill in the world in Indonesia, Bogasari, together with Salim. After diversifying into noodles and pasta, Bogasari looked to bread as the next vertical. Indosari was formed.

As it happened, Yap Sr was in the Indosari office in downtown Jakarta when I was there to meet with Wendy Yap. Apparently, he was there often to run through the spread of newspapers and, ever the trader, to monitor information on the Bloomberg terminal. At 85 then, Yap Sr needed help walking but the frailty of his legs was no indication of the vibrancy of his spirit. He was effusive in his praise of his daughter and all that she had achieved. For the owners of Bogasari, going into bread production was a natural extension of their core business. And Wendy Yap was the natural choice to head the new company.

She was 39 when she took the helm. While that may seem a tad youthful, age is but a number as far as this seasoned businesswoman is concerned. Yap started working for her father when she was 21, cutting her teeth in his real estate business in the US and later running the various family concerns in Indonesia in natural resources, real estate and food, including the American-based fast food franchise, Wendy's, in Indonesia in the 1990s. The association there can't be missed.

When I first met Yap, I was struck by her porcelain-fine skin and bright eyes that belied her 57 years. She was welcoming and wore a perpetual smile. She laughed easily and talked readily about her love for cooking (and eating) and her interest in fine wines. She even had a small kitchen in her office where she would whip up a quick meal between meetings, if time permitted. As for her wines, she had her vintages stored in various fine restaurants around the country.

But there the image of the leisurely *ibu,* or lady, ends. She was asked to chair a meeting among her staff for our cameras and, at the flick of a switch, her business persona was activated. She began asking pointed questions, listening intently, and giving clear directions. At one point, I began to wonder if she was even aware of the camera in the room. Taking control seemed second nature to her. How else could she have built the largest bread business in Indonesia, with a market capitalisation of about US$550 million, over two decades, without some fire in her belly?

Today, Sari Roti takes up 90% of market share in the mass market bread segment at home. It has 10 factories across the country, with five more coming onstream from 2019. The factories currently churn 4.2 million pieces of bread a day from its 60 production lines.

Discovering the Indonesian taste profile

The success of a food product would depend on a multitude of factors, but the proof of the pudding has to be, at the very least, in the eating. For fans of Sari Roti, it was the company's signature Japanese bread that got them hooked and sent the company's fortunes to the top of the table.

The Yap family was determined from the beginning that the soft texture of Japanese bread was the way to go. It helped that Yap loved Japanese bread, and she was not alone in the fan club. "I noticed that the Japanese style bakeries (in Singapore) will always sell out their breads… Plus the Japanese technology, I would say is second to none. Their standard of hygiene, their product standard, it's just excellent. That's why we went to them."

Getting Japanese machinery is expensive. But the standard we got was very satisfactory indeed.

Specifically, they pursued the owners of Shikishima Baking Company in Nagoya, Japan. In his memoirs, Yap Sr recalled, "It took a few years to convince the late Chairman Keikichi Morita to agree to this joint venture in Indonesia as he was concerned that the lack of quality control in Indonesia would affect Shikishima's reputation."[3]

Yap Sr understood the chairman's reservations as Shikishima was the oldest bread company in Japan, established in 1919, and quality was, naturally, foremost on their minds. But the Yap family's enthusiasm and influence, the backing of the Salim Group, the potential of the Indonesian market, and the assurance of quality wheat flour coming from the family's flour mill won over the Japanese.

Agreeing to the terms laid out by the Japanese, however, would be costly. Nevertheless, it was a price the Yaps were willing to pay. "It was expensive because getting Japanese machinery is expensive. But the standard we got was very satisfactory indeed," said Wendy Yap.

The adoption of the technology has also helped the company in its expansion. Indosari has been able to replicate the production process across all 10 factories, with 80% of it being automated. Not only has this helped reduce reliance on labour, but by minimizing handling, hygiene and standardisation in quality are also assured.

Today, Sari Roti carries 40 different products, ranging from white bread to pandan muffins and chicken-teriyaki-filled sweet bread. Finding the right flavour profile is a constant challenge. Once, thinking they could replicate another success story in Japan, Sari Roti introduced the all-time Japanese favourite red bean paste in their sweet breads. But the product tanked.

"It just was not selling," was all Yap could offer. After 18 months, that line was discontinued. This requisite trial period is required "because it takes time to promote it; it takes time to get it known to the market and then you've got to give it time to see if they really like it," Yap explained.

Fortunately for Indosari, there have been more hits than misses, and being in the market for 20 years has given them a good feel of Indonesians' favourite flavour — chocolate. To meet consumer demand, almost half the products Sari Roti churns from its factories contain chocolate. That chocolate bread also happens to be Yap's favourite is a happy coincidence.

> I found out that sliced bread without the crust, most Asians would like it.

Product development is an area that Yap enjoys and the reason is obvious. "I'm a carb person," she declared. "I love bread!" And decisions on new product lines are sometimes informed by her preferences.

"I don't like bread with crusts," Yap revealed. "So, when we launched the sandwich line, it was a big hit because it had fillings of blueberry jam, peanut butter, and chocolate. But it didn't have the crust."

And the verdict from customers? "Everybody liked that! So, I found out that sliced bread without the crust, most Asians would like it," Yap said.

The next trend to look out for, according to Yap, is the demand for healthier alternatives. Even though sweet bread is the flavour of the day for Indonesians, the head of Sari Roti is not discounting the possibility that the demand for sugar-reduced products may be in the horizon. "I travel just to see the new ideas, the new bread, and the taste," said Yap. She believes the worldwide trend of healthier alternatives "would happen in Indonesia at some point."

Straddling the vast hinterland

To reach consumers across the 16th largest country in the world, businesses in Indonesia rely broadly on two channels of distribution — traditional and modern trades. The modern trade refers to hypermarkets, supermarkets, and minimarts, scattered through main cities and towns, while the traditional trade includes mom-and-pop shops and neighbourhood grocery stores or *warungs*. The latter are often ignored by fast-moving consumer goods manufacturers because they are fragmented and hard to reach. However, Nielsen estimates that about 70% of the sales of fast-moving consumer goods in Indonesia come from these neighbourhood convenience stores whose very proximity to and relationship with their customers make the shop shelves an extension of the customers' kitchen pantry.[4]

> The distribution strategy is based on penetrating the middle income.

In 2014, traditional trade took up 30% of Indosari's distribution, and Yap was clear about raising the stakes there. With 50,000 outlets nationwide that year (the number of outlets has, since, increased to 67,000 in 2017), the head honcho estimated that she'd covered only about 10% of the market. So, one of the catalysts for growth is further penetration of the traditional trade.

Getting Sari Roti in the hands of people in the towns of this expansive archipelago of 2 million square kilometres and 6,000 inhabited islands would be no mean feat. The first challenge was to identify the customers. "The distribution strategy is based on penetrating the middle income," explained Yap, pointing out the large and growing segment in the country.

The next task was to make the breads last longer so that by the time it reaches the consumer, they would still be fresh. For that,

Indosari turned to their Japanese technology and equipment. The automated production process keeps human contact minimal, eliminating contaminants and the vacuum seals lock in the freshness in the packaging. In this way, their breads stay good for up to five days.

Now that it could last longer, the third challenge was to set up a network of factories and distributors right across this country of islands. The spread of production facilities in strategic locations close to its markets was the key. Within a few years from its first production, the factory in Cikarang in West Java reached its maximum capacity. Several lines of products were being pushed out of the plant. More had to be done — and fast.

In 2005, the second factory in East Java was set up about 700 kilometres away from the first. Since then, it's been about one factory a year to build the company's capacity and extend its reach. With the boost from its initial public offering in 2010, Indosari stamped its presence with 10 factories spread across the three most populous Indonesian islands of Java, Sumatra, and Sulawesi, in cities and towns with high concentration of the middle class. From Medan in the west to Makassar in the east, Indosari's factories are located across 4,000 kilometres of first tier cities to reach as many people as possible in between.

Setting up manufacturing facilities in Indonesia, however, can be a tedious process. Yap recalled a particularly trying episode just laying the groundwork for the factory in Palembang in South Sumatra. After identifying the market and earmarking a location central enough to serve it, Yap's team was stumped when they realised that basic utilities were lacking. The responsibility fell on the company to connect its own water and power supply. The task of dealing with the authorities and various agencies seemed so overwhelming at times, Yap thought the project would never take off. "I would say that probably was the riskiest venture," she revealed.

Chiming its way into neighbourhoods

The key to Sari Roti's dominance in Indonesia and the factor that makes its lead in the market almost unassailable is its unique distribution network. Back in the 1980s, US-based bakery Sara Lee had set up its Indonesian arm, and even by 1997, it was still building its capacity with a factory that could churn out 15,000 pieces a day. But it failed to get a foothold in the market.

At the risk of over-simplifying the reasons for Sara Lee's failure to launch itself into the big league in Indonesia, it's worth looking at what it lacked and where Indosari succeeded.

Apart from reaching out to low-hanging fruits like supermarkets and minimarts in cities and towns, Indosari relies on 3,000 mobile Sari Roti tricycle carts that ply the neighbourhoods in towns and cities, calling out to residents with the brand's signature jingle chiming from the tricycles' speakers.

Penetrating the traditional market can be a convoluted process. It entails the use of distributors and agents who, in turn, use their own agents. Hawkers are recruited to sell the breads in alleyways. "That's the way to penetrate the market, to make sure the bread is available and accessible everywhere in Indonesia," revealed Yap.

Through the use of neighbourhood hawkers on its tricycle carts, Indosari has gained an additional advantage. It's able to gather data on consumption patterns of specific households — from the quantity to the types of bread they buy.

Hawkers are motivated to feed the information back to their suppliers as the company runs on a no-returns policy, making the hawkers responsible for their own inventory. The short sell-by date of the bread ensures that they only take what they can sell.

At the same time, Indosari needs to make sure that the right quantity is supplied to the hawkers to prevent them from pushing expired bread just to clear their stock. Juggling 40 varieties of breads and cakes coming out of their factories throws even more challenges into the equation, and every form of inventory control is crucial.

Marketing local to locals

Indonesians trust local brands more than they do international ones "simply because consumers trust Indonesian companies, take pride in using local brands, and believe that local companies truly understand Indonesian consumers and provide better value for money when compared with foreign brands," according to a McKinsey report.[5] Riding on this sentiment, Sari Roti launched a marketing campaign in 2015, calling their loaves *The Bread of Indonesia*. It took its message to the hearts of Indonesians through traditional and digital advertising as well as through road shows at various consumer fairs in major towns throughout the country.

And to capture customers from young, the company takes its campaigns to schools and, of course, sells its products in school canteens. In the popular children's simulation theme park, Kidzania, in Jakarta, the bread maker has its own interactive station, Sari Roti House. There, children get to play the role of a baker. The engagement with its customers, both young and old, has reaped positive results. Sari Roti has consistently been the undisputed leader in the country's Top Brand Awards in the white bread category.

Caught in a political and religious maelstrom

For 20 years since its founding, Indosari has had a relatively smooth ride to growth. However, in late 2016, it got caught in the political and religious crossfire surrounding the incumbent Jakarta governor.[6] While Sari Roti rode the waves of the street protests of the 1997 Asian Financial Crisis to its advantage, the 212 protest, as it came to be known, proved to be a bane to the company.

It all began when Sari Roti vendors were photographed giving away free bread to protesters who gathered to demand the imprisonment of the Jakarta governor for blasphemy. The praise the company won among Muslims for its apparent generosity turned swiftly into calls for a boycott after Indosari stated the free distribution was not a corporate policy but the act of individuals.

The company's share price saw a dip during the outcry but rebounded within weeks. The thrashing it received from the incident led to a dent to its topline. In 2017, Indosari booked net sales of US$180 million, a 1% decline from the year before. Its lacklustre performance was all the more noteworthy after chalking a consistent growth rate of at least 16% in previous years.

Another factor leading to the static sales in 2017 was the price increase the company introduced that year. However in a recent interview with Forbes Indonesia, Yap expressed confidence that the worst was over and a 20% growth rate is on the horizon.[7] This optimism is fed, among other factors, by fund injections from a rights issue that raised US$100 million and a further US$90 million from private equity firm KKR in return for a 15% share of the company.

Facing the crossing

The coming years will be critical for Indosari as it crosses into new territories of diversification, overseas expansion and a more competitive domestic market.

A report by The Economist noted a trend among Africans eating like Asians as their rice consumption increases, while Asians are eating like Americans, pushing up the demand for wheat — particularly for bread.[8] As income levels rise in Indonesia, the sale of bread will move in tandem. To catch that wave, more players have jumped on the bandwagon to feed the demand. Most notable are those manufacturers that have links to large retail chains.

In 2014, Sumber Alfaria Trijaya, the company that runs one of the largest chains of minimarts in Indonesia roped in Japanese bread maker Yamazaki as a partner to produce their own bread. The bakery's aim is to supply to 4,000 Alfamart outlets for a start. The company has more than 10,000 stores throughout the country.

In late 2016, another player entered the market — Prime Bread. The owner of the brand, Gardenia Makmur Selaras, already has an established brand and operations in Singapore, Malaysia and the Philippines, with their top-selling bread, Gardenia. Another advantage Prime Bread has is ready access to Indonesia's largest chain of minimarts, Indomaret, simply because both brands and outlets share the same owner in Anthoni Salim of Salim Group (the Group, of course, also owns 25% of Indosari). With solid production experience and ready distribution channels, Prime Bread has sprinted out of the starting blocks and within a short period, is already selling in about 2,000 Indomaret outlets.

While more bread producers are entering the market, breaking into Indosari's strongholds won't be easy. The company's scale, distribution network, technology and branding have placed it in a dominant leadership position. In the meantime, Indosari plans to diversify to develop a chain of cafés and to acquire a majority share of a frozen dough producer to expand their market to include hotels, airlines and restaurants.

Even back in 2014 when we met and before the proliferation of new brands in the market, Yap was already intent on keeping her eye on the ball. "It's not good to remain complacent just because you're a

> It's not good to remain complacent just because you're a market leader.

market leader or you already have a brand," she said. "I think we have to keep moving up." And Indosari hasn't just kept moving up, it has moved out as well.

In 2016, Indosari made its first foray overseas — to the Philippines. A joint venture between Indosari and one of the Philippines' largest food manufacturer and distributor, Monde Nissin, was formed. The 55–45 partnership, Sarimonde Foods Corporation, with Indosari holding the majority, combines the production expertise of Indosari and Monde Nissin's wide distribution network. Shortly after the agreement was signed, the joint venture acquired Walter Bread, a 30-year-old brand from the Philippines.

Joining hands with another partner in 2017, this time in Korea, Indosari is set to supply cakes and pastries to over 500 outlets of the Korean coffee franchise, Caffe Bene — all in line with the grand plan to make Indosari Asia's leading bread producer by 2025.

Though its home market is huge enough to keep most contented, there are good reasons for Indosari not to live on bread for Indonesia alone. As more players enter the fray and margins get thinner, the push is there for it to expand further afield. It took 20 years for it to establish itself firmly at home. The next lap has to be about diversification and expansion overseas. While it's able to transfer its technology and production to a new territory relatively easily, it will, however, have to start with a new set of rules to grow its brands in new frontiers.

Notes

1 "Top 5 Emerging Markets with the Best Middle Class Potential", September 20, 2015, Euromonitor International, accessed 6 July 2017, <http://blog.euromonitor.com/2015/09/top-5-emerging-markets-with-the-best-middle-class-potential.html>

2 Rohit Razdan, Mohit Das and Ajay Sohoni, November 2013, "The top six things marketers need to know about the new Indonesian consumer" McKinsey & Company, accessed on 6 July 2017, <http://www.mckinsey.com/business-functions/marketing-and-sales/our-insights/the-top-six-things-marketers-need-to-know-about-the-new-indonesian-consumer>

3 Piet Yap, *The Grains of My Life*, Singapore, 2010, p184.

4   "The power of traditional trade grocery stores in the battle for market share", 15 October 2015, Nielson, accessed on 6 July 2017, <http://www.nielson.com/apac/en/insights/reports/2015/the-power-of-traditional-trade.html>

5   Rohit Razdan, Mohit Das and Ajay Sohoni, January 2014, "The evolving Indonesian consumer", McKinsey & Company, accessed 6 July 2017, <http://www.mckinsey.com/business-functions/marketing-and-sales/our-insights/the-evolving-indonesian-consumer>

6   "Sari Roti stock down amid boycott campaign", The Jakarta Post, 7 December 2016.

7   "10 inspiring women: Wendy Yap", Forbes Indonesia, April 2018.

8   "Of rice and men: A circular tale of changing food preferences", 11 March 2017, The Economist, accessed 8 July 2017, <https://www.economist.com/news/international/21718508-west-africans-are-eating-more-asians-asians-are-eating-more-americans-and>

With Mochtar Riady at the Mochtar Riady Institute of Nanotechnology in Lippo Karawaci, the Lippo Group's township where Pak Mochtar lives and works, in 2015.

With Balbina Wong (middle) and executive producer Huang Weixian (right) in Hong Kong, in 2013.

With John Gokongwei Jr. in Manila, in 2012.

With Roger Lee at his office showroom in Hong Kong, in 2015.

With Anand Mahindra in Mumbai, in 2015.

Having a meal with Francis Yeoh at his specially curated local foodcourt, Hutong,
at Lot 10, Kuala Lumpur, in 2014.

With Chanda Kochhar at ICICI's headquarters in Mumbai, in 2014.

Taking a ride in a Grab car with Tan Hooi Ling in Singapore, in 2016.

Trying to keep up with Tony Lo around Giant's factory in Taichung, Taiwan, in 2016.

With Deep Kalra in Gurugram, India, in 2015

With Anupam Mittal in his penthouse in Mumbai, in 2014.

With Schauna Chauhan in Mumbai, in 2013.

With Tony Fernandes at the former AirAsia Academy in Sepang, Malaysia, in 2014.

Chatting before the interview with Wendy Yap (middle) and her father, cofounder of Bogasari, Piet Yap (right), in Jakarta, in 2014.

Admiring the Botero sculpture with Tahir in his home in Sentosa, Singapore, in 2013.

Part V

TECH UPSTARTS

No discussion of movers and shakers in Asia can preclude the founders of technology startups. The new age businesses of these young titans have fundamentally changed the way we live, entertain, relax, move, and even make our most intimate of choices. Asia today boasts 75 unicorns that are valued from US$1 billion each — that's about 30% of the global share[1] and much of the activity really only began in the last five years. Despite the fact that 90% of startups fail,[2] more people are fed by the success stories of unicorns than the fodder that comes from the failures. While the ambition of Generation X was to find prestige from employment with large multinationals, millennials are forsaking the path most travelled by their parents, to go out on a limb as tech entrepreneurs. With Asia's ballooning young population, the opportunities presented by technology, the low barriers to entry and the pool of investors, flushed with cash and ready to invest in that next big idea, this trend is set to continue for some time yet.

The challenge most startup founders have is introducing ideas so revolutionary that much of their time in the early stages is spent showing people *how* to use their services. The rate of growth must be nothing short of exponential for investors to even want to consider putting money in the entity. The gold standard investors typically look for is a user take up rate of 5–7% a week, according to startup guru and angel investor Paul Graham.[3]

While I'm always intrigued by the tenacity and self-belief of successful entrepreneurs who insist that people need a service they don't even know about, I'm also just as curious to learn how they stay the course with the whirlwind momentum of their companies' growth. And what of companies that have gone past the stage of growth to maturity, how do founders navigate their way through this unfamiliar territory of plateaus and (God forbid!) declines?

Following are stories of pioneers in their industry who are still on the incline and those who've necessarily moved on to the stage of consolidation. No other time in history has the world witnessed companies that have grown by such exponential proportions. But therein lies lessons in the fortitude of the human spirit — buoyed and ravaged by explosive growth, what remains when the dust settles?

Chapter 12

The Chinese Internet Pioneer

Charles Zhang
Sohu.com, China

I n the Chinese digital sphere, the giants of BAT have a formidable presence. Representing the trio of Baidu, Alibaba and Tencent, the three companies dominate the internet space with over US$50 billion in sales collectively in 2016. As if the domestic market was not enough, Alibaba and Tencent have notably scoured the globe for acquisitions to widen their share of the market. From micro-blogging, e-commerce, and payment systems, the giants' appetites are insatiable. And growth momentum isn't slowing down. In 2016, Alibaba and Tencent registered remarkable upticks in sales by 56% and 48% respectively.[4]

Missing in all the hubbub is the search giant, Baidu, also known as the Google of China. Its growth stumbled in 2016 after negative publicity from the death of a student who sought treatment for cancer from an advertisement on their platform. Regulators came down hard on Baidu, tightening the rules on online advertising, their bread and butter.

Another reason for Baidu's slower growth is its lag in jumping on the mobile bandwagon. Online advertisers have begun to look beyond search ads to popular social media networks like WeChat, which belongs to Tencent, and e-commerce platforms, where Alibaba dominates. Baidu's lack of presence in these areas is seeing its clients shifting their advertising dollar away from the search giant.

While Baidu has placed its bets on Artificial Intelligence, whose outcomes will not be evident for years to come, the question arises whether it will be toppled off the podium for what one observer termed as its "lack of innovation and series of management blunders,"[5] a description that's reminiscent of an internet pioneer who rose to the pinnacle of the digital economy in China only to become a secondary player in the scene today. Could Baidu and other players in the business take a leaf out of Sohu's book to avert the possibility of a steep decline?

Let it be known that secondary players in China's digital economy don't handle small change in a sphere that contributed 30% to China's GDP in 2016, or US$3.35 trillion.[6] Sohu, a search, media and gaming company, is worth over US$2 billion in market capitalisation and was one of the first internet companies in China, with its beginnings in China's own introduction to the internet in 1996. While it soared in its early years and its founder became the model of internet entrepreneurship, Sohu failed to catch on with innovations and slipped off its pole position.

Sohu's growth has remained stable over the years while its other peers have soared to dizzying heights. It raked in US$1 billion in revenue in 2016 primarily from advertising, while its search engine, Sogou, is the third most popular in China and its online gaming business, Changyou, is one of the country's leading massively multiplayer online games developer and operator.

The study of the meteoric rise and plateau of Charles Zhang, the founder of Sohu, depicts the frenetic pace of China's internet space, the mettle needed to thrive in that business, the agility and foresight to get in on trends (or be lost) and the requisite compliance in dealing with regulators in a country known for its Great Firewall.

So, who is Sohu?

Our attempts to nail the interview with Zhang hit several speed bumps. His publicist gave the impression that he was interested to meet but he proved elusive each time we settled on a date. When we finally did get a date to meet in Singapore where he was making a stopover to attend to his new venture in luxury yachts, we were stalled again for no apparent reason at the very last minute. Another date was set and this time the stars aligned in 2014 in Beijing.

We met at the Sohu.com Media Centre, the company's own building in the Silicon Valley of Beijing. Zhang's penthouse office was cavernous with attached board room, living area, bathroom and balcony — very likely a second home for the bachelor. He even has a coffee counter, complete with a barista.

When Zhang emerged from his office to the living area where the interview was set up, I was met by a man, slightly built, who could've passed off as one a decade younger than his 50 years. This was the man who pioneered the tech start-up scene in China even before the term was coined, when the concept of a venture capitalist was as alien as the internet. Instead of a flamboyant firebrand, as most reports had made him out to be, he turned out a little reserved and awkward, even. He was tentative initially but got more comfortable as he settled in to our conversation. He admitted that he hardly reads or watches interviews he's given (but promised to give this one a go).

My goal was to get beyond the surface to understand what made this techpreneur as audacious as he was in an environment, that, 20 years ago, was strait-laced and ignorant of the technological breakthroughs happening on the other side of the world, in the US. I wanted to go beyond the headlines to hear his take on where and how he fell short along the way. Of course, I was also piqued by stories I had read about Zhang's relationship with Chinese movie A-listers such as Zhang Ziyi and how he brought the company to the global stage as the sponsor of internet services in the 2008 Beijing Olympics. He also made the news for scaling the heights of Mount Everest before plummeting to the depths of depression that led to him to a year-long sabbatical.

An internet wilderness

I was the only one trying to do something that nobody understood.

Zhang started Internet Technologies China (ITC), which he later renamed Sohu.com, in 1996 after returning from the US where he was the liaison officer for China at Massachusetts Institute of Technology (MIT), his alma mater. He had graduated with a PhD in experimental physics. At that time, the Chinese economy was driven by state-owned industries in banking, oil and gas, and infrastructure.

"I was the only one trying to do something that nobody understood," recalled Zhang of the early days when he began work on the first Chinese online service. Sohu.com provided online advertisement and shopping, website design, and technical assistance. It also enabled users to send text messages from their mobile phones. These were remarkable advances at a time when the internet backbone network had just been completed in China and network services were only beginning to be rolled out throughout the country.[7]

Zhang has his stay in the US to thank for being the visionary that he was in China. "In the early days, I returned from the US and I had access to MIT and few US friends who had money. And knowing English and getting access to the information about what's going on in the US with Yahoo, America Online, all about the internet — this access to knowledge and access to capital and connections helped."

One of those "friends" included the founder of the MIT's Media Lab, Nicholas Negroponte, who introduced him to venture capitalists. Sohu.com became the first internet company in China to receive venture capital, a term no one had even heard about there. Even Yahoo's Jerry Yang knocked on Zhang's door for merger talks.

But there was still one major impediment at home — the services offered by Sohu.com to the Chinese were so revolutionary that it was beyond the understanding of most. After all, it was only a year before Sohu.com was launched that the internet began its first roll-out nationwide. Zhang could see the many uses of it because the online space was already abuzz in the US, but to the Chinese, fixed-line telephone communication then was enough of a luxury. So, the most needful thing he had to do to ensure Sohu's survival was to start building awareness.

"I actually did a lot of interviews and basically talked to the media and got the word out. So, I created a lot of publicity," he recalled.

That publicity included appearing half naked on the cover of a magazine as a gangster rapper and skateboarding through Tiananmen Square. It all worked out well as *Time* magazine named Zhang one of the top 50 cyber elites in 1998 and *Fortune* listed him one of the top 25 new corporate stars in 2001. His lavish lifestyle of luxury cars and yachts was much-publicised, and he once even said, "If it is not the most luxurious and expensive yacht in China, its meaning is lost to me."[8]

As Zhang became China's first internet celebrity, Sohu.com's fortunes rose in tandem as it became the top internet company in the country. It listed on Nasdaq in 2000, taking him into the *Forbes'* rich list in China.

For all his flamboyance and swagger, Zhang was anything but ill-disciplined. Taking his cue from his mentors in the US, he started what he called "bottom-line thinking."

"I have a very strong sense of crisis and I always really do the basic things. I was not easily excited," he explained. "I would look at things with a really cool mind so that in the process of raising money, establishing a board, having the right product, doing the right marketing strategy, it was all about how to spend the minimum amount of money to achieve maximum effect."

Achieving the multiplier effect

Zhang believed the low barriers to entry in the internet business was the trigger to the industry's exponential growth. Anyone could start a website. Traditional resources such as capital, land, permits, and bank loans were no longer needed.

> As long as this product is better than your competitors by 20% or 30%, the reward by the users will be by several hundred percent or even exploding to a thousand percent.

"Even if you don't have these linear resources, but you have some limited, minimum resources, or just some ideas, you can start a website. And as long as this product is better than your competitors by 20% or 30%, the reward by the users will be by several hundred percent or even exploding to a thousand percent. That means the traffic grows non-linearly," Zhang explained.

All this, thanks to the burgeoning number of internet users in China which has been seeing double digit growth since 2012. In 2016, more than half the population in China, or in excess of 700 million users, have gone online.[9]

The easy accessibility into the industry and asset-light nature of the online business have created a level playing field for local start-ups pitting themselves against the global giants. For Zhang, it was all about the best idea and service that will lead to what he called "market selection." It was, in other words, a consumer-driven business from the beginning.

"It's not how much money you have, even how much technology you have; you write your own software anyway." Zhang goes on to explain, "It's like you taking some people to the ocean to see who swims the best. And you think you know because, oh, this one is strong, this one is tall. You decide? No, you don't decide. You just drive them to the ocean and the one that survives the longest is the fittest and the strongest." Foreign competitors entering the Chinese space, Zhang maintained, can't outdo the local champions just because of their global size and presence. Knowledge of the market and the ability to work with the authorities are paramount.

A case in point is Google China. Its run-ins with the Chinese government over censorship issues have been well documented since it started operations there in 2004. Searches of sensitive issues relating to China were consistently blocked until 2010, when the American company decided to pull out its search service from China after its Gmail accounts were hacked. It may seem that Google had taken the high moral ground in its decision to withdraw from the Chinese market. It refused to bow to Chinese censorship, staying true to their corporate slogan, *Don't Be Evil.* But many observers maintain that Google had lost ground long before its withdrawal because it failed to understand the Chinese user.[10]

Zhang, too, felt unconcerned about foreign competition. Using Facebook, which was blocked in 2009, as an example, he insisted that the American social media giant would've failed in China anyway. The inability to grasp market sentiment in China has been the Achilles heel of many a foreign company wanting a slice of the giant pie in the country.

The Great Firewall

I can't answer the question.

Online service providers in China are bound by law to preclude "socially destabilizing content," which is code for anything that undermines the state's authority. At the time I was scheduled to meet Zhang in 2014, the Occupy Central protest that paralysed Hong Kong's financial district for weeks was ongoing. Students in the Special Administrative Region gathered to protest against China's control over Hong Kong's electoral system. Information on the protest was blocked over the internet in China.

When I asked Zhang if he had been told to keep news of the protest out of his websites, he stumbled on his response and in a muted tone: "I can't… I can't answer the question." When pressed to explain his responsibility to users on providing information without discretion, he pulled out the song sheet that many Chinese internet entrepreneurs sing from.

"I can't answer you. I mean, it's national policy. But if you look at the vast area of information and the lifestyle and others, I think we are enjoying much more content information than before," Zhang offered. The operative words being *more… than before.*

A closer look at the generation of internet titans in China, the likes of Robin Li, Jack Ma, Pony Ma, and Charles Zhang, will reveal their growing years during the Cultural Revolution amid poverty and persecution. These became known as the Suffering Generation, born between 1960 and 1970. They've seen destitution and have come to wealth they could not have imagined.

Even as the economy opened its doors to global trade and they were given the reins to explore and expand their creativity and entrepreneurship, these internet bigwigs have the 1989 crackdown in Tiananmen Square to constantly remind them of the heavy hand of the government, an iron fist in a velvet glove. Their pragmatism is also tempered by the extremes in wealth and poverty they've experienced and the weight of stewardship as forerunners of China's prosperity. So, while outsiders may criticise Chinese internet entrepreneurs for their self-censorship and ready compliance to the authorities, the experience of that generation informs them in more complex and nuanced ways than left-wing critics can ever come to appreciate.

Losing the plot

Ironically, being a pioneer himself, Zhang learnt the advantage of the first mover as a laggard. Over the years, on his admission, he failed to

> I should have spent more time really understanding the internet landscape and how the ecosystem of the internet was developing.

keep his eye on the ball. In the early days, Sohu.com had contracted a little-known company to power its search index. As search began to gain traction, that company decided to launch its own service, rather than enrich others with it. Today its founder, Robin Li, is one of China's richest men from the company he started — Baidu.

Zhang felt that he had the rug pulled out from under him. "I spent a lot of time doing marketing. And at that time, I should have spent more time really understanding the internet landscape and how the ecosystem of the internet was developing. I should've really focused on search," he conceded.

Of course, Baidu became a runaway success with giants such as Google, Yahoo, and Microsoft making bids for the company. It is today the fourth most popular website in the world. Instead of being the leader, Sohu.com found itself in the game of catch-up, coming up with its search engine Sogou.com four years after Baidu.

As if that wasn't a hard-enough lesson, Zhang faced another disappointment a few years later. At that time, Sohu.com was working on a social networking site along the lines of Facebook. But before it could be launched, Sina Weibo, China's version of Twitter, burst onto the scene in August 2009. Within two months, Sina garnered 50 million users and today remains the most popular microblogging site in China. Charles Chao, the founder of Sina, snapped up the opportunity to launch Sina Weibo when the Chinese government clamped down on Twitter and its Chinese copy, Fanfou, in anticipation of the 20th anniversary of the Tiananmen massacre.

"Sina was a media company like us in the early days," Zhang recalled. "So, when their microblog exploded, we were afraid that it would render our media services obsolete. We had to catch up and change our strategy by switching from developing a Facebook-type service to developing *weibo* (microblogging) to compete with Sina." Sohu Weibo was launched soon after but has never been a real contender. It was this final pursuit to keep up with the intense competition that finally broke Zhang.

He sunk into depression.

Zhang took a year off and has said little about the experience apart from an interview that he gave just as he was about to return to work. He revealed that he was often gripped with fear and had no way to deal with them. He couldn't reconcile how he felt with the way the world saw him: "I think there's something wrong with me. I truly have everything, and yet I am so miserable. Happiness is totally unrelated to how much money you have."[11] Zhang said he sought treatment in the US and read books on spirituality and philosophy during his time away.

When I asked about the episode, he was reluctant initially to talk about that chapter in his life, telling me to "wait for my book." But when I probed further and asked what he had learnt from the whole episode, he revealed that he had grown to be a better leader.

> I think people need to be humble. Then you can think things more clearly.

"Before the depression started, I was sometimes arrogant and sometimes thought that I was such a great person. And sometimes when you think that way, you lose your ground. And I think people need to be humble. Then you can think things more clearly. So, I think I have become much more humble," Zhang said, before adding, "More humble than before."

"When I talk to people and have meetings and study the subject," Zhang went on to explain, "I'm not clouded or shielded by my own fame and self-importance. I see things more clearly, more thoroughly. So, it helps me to understand things better. I just put myself aside. And this helps. And I can see that I can think more clearly and make more high-quality decisions."

Since returning to run the company after his sabbatical, Zhang has presided over a stable topline. But operating costs have been outstripping revenue with 2017 seeing a loss of US$209 million. The company acknowledges that the way to stay ahead is to develop new products and services. What these numbers point to is slower growth in the company and it might even suggest a change of strategy is in order.

In 2015 Zhang put up an offer of US$600 million to buy back shares from Sohu in a move that's a prelude to privatisation. The financing committee rejected the proposal. A year later in 2017, Zhang made another offer. This time, a 50% premium to buy back Changyou, its subsidiary, also listed on Nasdaq. This follows the trend of Chinese companies delisting in the US in recent years as they see their shares undervalued there.

Obviously, Zhang is still very much in the game, wrestling back control to grow the company further. In relative terms, he may not be a headline grabber as in the past, but in absolute terms, who can dispute the influence of a man who runs a company that has over 500 million active users and a market capitalisation of over US$2 billion. Perhaps the hunger for the top spot is no longer an obsession; perhaps the drubbing he's received from competitors has grounded him to a point of being, dare I say, mellow.

But it'll be foolhardy to count Zhang out of the internet scene altogether. The clout and the experience he's gathered over two decades stands him in good stead. Can Zhang be as successful in regaining lost ground as he was pioneering the radical change in the lifestyles of the Chinese? In his own words, only the fittest and the ones with the staying power can survive the ocean of turbulence and ever-changing tides.

No rest for the weary in China's cyberspace.

Notes

1 Sadachika Watnabe, "Asia now home to 75 unicorns as sharing economy takes off", Nikkei Asian Review, 4 December 2017, <https://asia.nikkei.com/Business/Trends/Asia-now-home-to-75-unicorns-as-sharing-economy-takes-off>

2 Neil Patel, "90% Of Startups Fail: Here's What You Need To Know About The 10%", Forbes, 16 January 2015, <https://www.forbes.com/sites/neilpatel/2015/01/16/90-of-startups-will-fail-heres-what-you-need-to-know-about-the-10/#5d2822c66679>

3 Paul Graham, "Startup = Growth", paulgraham.com, September 2012, <http://www.paulgraham.com/growth.html>

4 Leo Sun, "Forget FANG; Buy BAT: Baidu, Alibaba, and Tencent", The Motley Fool 17 June 2017, <https://www.fool.com/investing/2017/06/17/forget-fang-buy-bat-baidu-alibaba-and-tencent.aspx>

5 "China's internet giants go global", The Economist, 20 April 2017 <https://www.economist.com/news/business/21721203-tencent-leading-acquisition-spree-alibaba-close-second-chinas-internet-giants-go>

6 "China's digital economy surges 18.9%, drives growth", Chinadaily.com.cn, 20 July 2017, <http://europe.chinadaily.com.cn/business/2017-07/20/content_30179877.htm>

7 Hu Weiwei, "The Internet Timeline of China 1987–1996", China Radio International, 19 March 2009.

8 A "China's internet users grew in 2016 by the size of Ukraine's population to 731 million", South China Morning Post, 22 January 2017, <https://cnnic.com.cn/IDR/hlwfzdsj/201306/t20130628_40563.htm>

9 In an interview with Bloomberg, Baidu's founder, Robin Li, cited these statistics. "Even before they announced they (Google) were giving up on China, we had 70% of the market. Google came in to China in 2005. At that time their market share was about 30%. By the end of 2009 when they were about to give up, their market share was in their teens. They lost money for 5 years. They ran out of patience, I guess." Li's more pointed analysis of Google's loss was expressed at a question-and-answer session at the Asia Financial Forum in Hong Kong in 2014. He pointed out that foreign internet companies have not been able to establish a foothold in China because of their unfamiliarity with the market and, indeed, the naivety of their knowledge of the Chinese user. Right off the bat, Google barked up the wrong tree, Li says. "The Chinese name of Google is, gu ge," explains Li. "Gu means 'grains' and ge means 'song'. Together the words mean 'a song of harvest'. They thought people would feel happy about a good harvest. But the netizens in China couldn't care less about any harvest."

10 Yang Lan Official Channel, <https://www.youtube.com/watch?v=4t6Q0BTgKhI&t=374s>

Chapter 13

The Ride of Their Lives

Bhavish Aggarwal* and Tan Hooi Ling[†]
*Ola, India
[†]Grab, Singapore

I t was the tech guru himself, the late Steve Jobs, who decried the veracity of focus group discussions because "people don't know what they want until you show it to them."

Nowhere is this more evident than the arrival of ride-hailing services in Asia, where safety and a lack of transportation options were common bugbears for decades. With apps like Grab available throughout Southeast Asia, and Ola in India, almost overnight the transportation landscape changed drastically. Rides can now be tracked, drivers held accountable and commuters can hop on to all manner of city transportation in the form of cars, motorbikes or auto rickshaws. For drivers, they need no longer wander around in an empty cab looking for passengers, while the low barriers to entry also means anyone who owned a decent enough car could earn extra income as drivers of their own vehicles. A win-win-win solution for all.

Grab and Ola are the shining examples of unicorns in Asia, much sought after by blue chip investors like Softbank, Sequoia, and Tiger Global, each wanting a slice of their pies in the huge markets that are their playing fields. Ola is valued at US$7 billion, while Grab is a shade less at US$6 billion. Valuations, of course, are mere estimates but both companies claim profitability in some form. Not bad for entities that are relatively young. Ola began operations in 2011 in Bangalore and Grab a year later in Kuala Lumpur. In fact, in projections filed with the Indian authorities, Ola is likely to rake in an operating profit of US$180 million by FY2019.[1] My interviews with the co-founders of the two companies show distinct similarities in the way each started their journey and the motivation that drives them to continue innovating, a euphemism for the paranoia that keeps them constantly looking over their shoulders.

Find a need, meet it

Both Bhavish Aggarwal and Tan Hooi Ling were brilliant students — Aggarwal graduated from India's top university, the Indian Institute of Technology Bombay and Tan from Harvard Business School. Both were quickly snapped up by multinationals and both found themselves giving up the regular pay check for their entrepreneurial journey. Interestingly, Aggarwal and Tan come from families who have no backgrounds in business. At least not in the last couple of generations. Tan hails from a middle-class family in Kuala Lumpur; her father is an engineer and mother, a remisier. Aggarwal comes from a line of doctors and engineers. If he had to find the entrepreneur in his bloodline, it would be in his caste lineage as a *bania* or the caste of businessmen. "Not that I believe in the caste system," disclaimed Aggarwal, "but I think these things probably skipped through generations. So, when I started off Ola, my parents actually said, 'My son has become a travel agent!'" referring to Olatrip, the online travel booking service he started off with.

Aggarwal carries himself with quiet confidence. He walked unobtrusively into the meeting room where the interview was set up. He appears almost tentative and self-deprecating. Not at all like what you'd imagine one of India's youngest billionaires to be. The Ola office is not outlandish like some startups I've seen in Singapore and the US. Purely functional, is how I'd describe it. Pretty much like the co-founder himself, who, to this day, proudly declares he doesn't own a car.

Olatrip was Aggarwal's first business venture after leaving Microsoft, a company he joined upon graduation. The venture lasted

> **You can't get too passionately in love with your idea. You have to also make a real business.**

a total of four months before the writing appeared on the wall. "That was the time when the Commonwealth Games were happening in India — in 2010 — and me and my co-founder (Ankit Bhati) used to stand outside the venues distributing the pamphlets hoping somebody would buy something. In the end, we hardly sold anything," he recalled.

While one idea began to fade, another took root. "While I was doing this travel business, we realised a lot of customers were asking us about fulfilling their transportation needs. So, we had, luckily, an ear to the ground, and then, we just flipped as soon as we could, because there was no other option in those early days. You can't get too passionately in love with your idea. You have to also make a real business," Aggarwal pointed out.

India has one of the lowest car ownership numbers in the world. In 2010, when Aggarwal began exploring the idea of a transportation business, there were 8 cars for every 1,000 people.[2] Seven years later in 2017, the number has increased four-fold to 32 per 1,000.[3] As significant an increase as this may be, there's still more demand than supply, and Ola is happy to fill the gap.

"People are not owning cars, so, what are they doing? [They] are moving in buses, all overcrowded buses, overcrowded local trains, overcrowded auto rickshaws. India is a very supply-constrained market on transportation. So, there's an opportunity for us to build a future of mobility using all the modern technologies for the Indian market. And, as we invent, as we made the pivot, it slowly, incrementally, dawned on us how big an opportunity this is," said Aggarwal.

From a more personal perspective, however, there were also "pain points" that needed to be medicated. "I've had many bad transportation experiences on multiple types of transportation — be it bus travel, be it inter-city car travel. And, if you think of India in 2010, the default way of getting around cities was auto rickshaws. And, in most Indian cities, actually, there are no medallion taxis, except for maybe Mumbai and Calcutta. So, it was a huge consumer need that I felt myself."

Meanwhile, thousands of kilometres away in Kuala Lumpur, it was a different problem that Tan Hooi Ling had to deal with in city transportation, a very real and personal issue. "I used to work as a

> We both realised we had an idea that we couldn't say no to because it had the potential of impacting so many lives of fellow Malaysians that we cared about.

consultant with McKinsey in my younger years, where I used to have to work really late hours, and the only way I could get myself back from the client office to home would be to take a taxi because even my mom, who's my personal chauffeur, would not stay up until 1 or 2 a.m. to take me home. And it was a very harrowing decision for us as a family because we knew it was not safe," Tan related.

Over the years, crimes perpetrated by taxi drivers in Kuala Lumpur have proliferated, causing much alarm and fear among commuters. As a resident of the city relying on public transportation, Tan and her mother came up with their own manual tracking solution. "I would actually text her my car details, who my driver was, what time I'd left, my estimated time of arrival. And I'll even share with her specific points, like 'I'm two minutes away, at this light stop, just outside Pizza Hut,' because that was the situation," Tan explained.

This led to conversations a few years later with her coursemate at Harvard Business School and future business partner, Anthony Tan, who also happened to be Malaysian. Why not leverage off technology to solve the problem? The idea grew into a conviction. "We both realised we had an idea that we couldn't say no to because it had the potential of impacting so many lives of fellow Malaysians that we cared about," she said.

And both knew that if anything was to come out of it, they had to be disciplined. They enrolled in a business plan competition at the university, which compelled them to work within timeframes. The process also gave them access to advisors that they would otherwise not get to hear from. The idea won the duo the second prize in the competition. From there, MyTeksi, Grab's earlier brand, was birthed.

Needless to say, as with all startups, their beginnings were humble and their roles, all-encompassing. Tan recalled Grab's first round of funding — a princely sum of US$25,000, which "at that point in time sounded like a lot of money." Aggarwal and his partner began with a paltry US$3,000 of their own seed money. Seeking financing initially was a challenge for Ola. "The toughest financing that I've ever faced was my angel round," recalled Aggarwal. "I remember meeting at least 50 angels, out of which, eventually, four gave me money."

Early investors have reaped more than their share of returns from betting on Ola and Grab. And as with all growth stories, their triumphs were tampered with trials.

Grab's disruption

While ride-hailing apps have won the day for drivers and commuters alike, parties with vested interests in the status quo and who've lost out have not gone quietly into the night. Taxi drivers who have for years operated under traditional public transportation licenses and have had their livelihoods stripped from them almost overnight brought their protests to the streets of Kuala Lumpur and Jakarta. They even harassed drivers of ride-hailing services and damaged their cars. Unions and groups supporting traditional transportation services lobbied the government to put an end to the service. The most drastic measure was seen in Indonesia in November 2015, when the transport minister announced a ban on all ride-hailing apps in the country, only to back paddle a day later and be reprimanded by the President after.

> We knew that positive change was coming because finally we're becoming a conversation that was worth having.

For Tan, confronting these issues is all in a day's work. After all, one doesn't start a revolution to be cowered by opposition. "Disruption is a more drastic way of talking about change," she mused. "Every time you have change, it's uncomfortable. And since the day we started at MyTeksi, we've brought change."

And Tan's response to the ban when it was first announced? "What was going on in my mind was 'Ah! This job never gets dull!' There's always a different challenge every single day," she remarked wryly. "So, when that set of news came out, we knew that things were changing. We knew that positive change was coming because, finally, we're becoming a conversation that was worth having. And as you saw with the overturn in the decision, we also had faith in the local government and local leaders that they wanted the same ultimate end goal that we do, which is safer transportation at a more accessible price, with less congestion. And that's exactly the same problem that we have been trying to deal with at Grab," she said.

Whether she's well-trained in PR spiel or she's naturally given to being phlegmatic, Tan mindfully steers clear of controversy. She would not reveal the hardest country to operate in, of the eight in Southeast Asia that Grab is present in; nor would she cast aspersions on rebel-rousing taxi drivers giving Grab a hard time. Tan displays a calmness, patience, and diplomacy that makes her a good spokesperson, a hardy leader in times of crises, and a good negotiator with the authorities — traits that stand her in good stead to navigate through the minefield of radical innovation.

One of the landmines ride-hailing companies find themselves confronted with is the complaint that they operate without much legislation and drivers are unencumbered by the rules that govern traditional taxi drivers. Working with the regulators to create a new transportation environment has been an on-going process of fits and starts, and operating in eight different countries means there are a lot of regulations to meander through.

"When we first launched our GrabCar services in Singapore, we had the same set of conversations with the LTA (Land Transport Authority), which is 'Hey folks, we have a good idea and a better solution to the transport needs in Singapore and because it's new, there is no regulatory structure around it right now.

> We've data to show that we've way more passengers, way more demand than any of our existing services could supply.

That being said, we know that we, and you, the LTA, share the same end goal. Let's start this conversation now to figure out what is the best regulatory infrastructure.' And in due time, that setup was created jointly over our conversations," explained Tan.

"That same process of creating something new, innovating, showing value, bringing data to the table of how we're improving lives, has happened in the Philippines, in Vietnam, and most of the other countries that we've worked with. In the Philippines, we're the very first company to actually have private hire vehicles licensed. In

Vietnam, we're the only company that is in an official partnership with the local government, because they understand where our goals lie, how we operate, what we ultimately want to do. We're all local tax-paying entities and therefore, our success is also their success," said Tan, like a seasoned negotiator.

In 2015, Grab established an R&D centre in Singapore and soon after moved its headquarters there. Driving the discussions among the team and giving them the motivation to push the envelope is the basic conviction that comes from numbers. "We have data to show that we've way more passengers, way more demand than any of our existing services could supply. So during peak periods, especially in the morning and afternoon, you'll never be able to get any cars, be it a taxi or a car, because there's so much demand. So, that's the data we use to say 'Hey, let's increase the avenues of supply because we know that that's what all our drivers and passengers need,'" said Tan.

Where there're risks and challenges, the rewards are also aplenty. For instance, while there've been on-going discussions with Indonesian regulators who recently proposed limits in tariffs and fleet sizes of online ride services, there's also been much to smile about there. "I will say that Indonesia is our fastest growing market by far, in terms of revenue, market share, everything. It is actually our most nascent market. We only entered a year and a half ago (in June 2014) and already our services have ballooned and exploded."

Grab is available in 100 cities in Indonesia and there are no plans to slow down. It provides rides by car and motorbike, the latter being a very popular source of transportation in the clogged roads of its capital, Jakarta. The company continues to keep its figures close to its heart but it's not hard to figure out how well it's doing. In a study by Google and Singapore's sovereign wealth fund, Temasek, Indonesia is and will continue to be the largest market for online rides in Southeast Asia up to 2025 and will be worth US$5.6 billion then.[4] And that's something Grab can smile about as a dominant player sharing the pie with local operator Go-Jek.

Until early 2018, US-based Uber was a strong contender in Indonesia with a formidable global presence. Its financial muscle of US$69 billion in valuation and its presence in over 80 countries dwarfs Ola and Grab combined. But it has had a patchy track record in Asia, particularly in Southeast Asia and in China. In 2016, it had to concede defeat and merge with the Chinese forerunner Didi Chuxing, then in April 2018, Grab announced that it, too, had bought over Uber's operations in Southeast Asia. Uber's exit in these markets, however, now means it has more resources to clue in on the next biggest market in the world — India.

Ola's bumpy road ahead

Uber's ousted CEO and founder, Travis Kalanick, had made no bones about setting his sights on India as his next battleground. It's been in the country since 2013 in 28 cities with 450,000 drivers. It's fearless in taking on the Indian incumbent, Ola. In its latest move to attract more drivers, Uber offered free life and accident insurance to its drivers, a benefit not widely available in many countries it operates in. But India is a different ball game.

The Uber vs. Ola competition has been fierce. Both companies claim frontrunner position.[5] There've been accusations levelled at each for flouting rules and tampering with the other's operations. Uber threw down the gauntlet when it set up dedicated technology centres in Hyderabad and Bangalore and promised investments of US$2 billion in the country.[6]

While Aggarwal attempted to be magnanimous in sharing the gargantuan pie that is India, claiming "the more the merrier," the generosity soon fizzled off as he declared that there can only be one winner.

> Ola versus Uber in India is like the Vietnam War... We are local guerrillas, Uber is the American company carpet bombing the country.

"Ola versus Uber in India is like the Vietnam War. We are the local guerrillas, and, I mean this as an analogy, and not anything war-related," Aggarwal qualified before continuing. "We are local guerrillas, Uber is the American company carpet bombing the country. But, we know the nooks and corners of the country, we know customer preferences, we know partner driver preferences, we know what kind of plan we have to build, we know what kind of technology we have to build. And that will enable us to win in the long term."

When I brought up the accusation by Uber against Ola in 2016 for setting up fraudulent accounts and booking 400,000 fake rides on Uber resulting in the global giant losing over 20,000 frustrated drivers,

Aggarwal found it hard to hold back his cynicism. "It's very clear what kind of a persona, globally, one company has. The kind of stuff going on with them around the world, it just shows the kind of culture, personality that company has," he said, referring to the controversies surrounding Uber's founder which led to his ouster in 2017.

When I tried getting closer to the raw nerve, Aggarwal regained his stance and bridged his response to the company's focus on the opportunities rather than the competition.

In a country of 1.3 billion people, with 28 states and seven union territories, each with its own government, operating a business across borders in India requires nimbleness and local know-how. What's permitted in one state doesn't necessarily work in another and being able to traverse the differences and keep abreast of regulations is a full-time job — particularly since Ola operates in 110 cities across India. Aggarwal learnt this in 2015, four years after starting Ola, when the government in Delhi declared that 80% of Ola and Uber cabs did not have valid licenses in the state.[7] Drivers with permits from neighbouring states and even all-India permits were suddenly told that they were illegally operating in Delhi.

> Working at a startup, you need to work without dogma... It's not just a work environment of managing the ship, because the ship is not there!

So, working with the authorities and building awareness is part of Aggarwal's job description. "A core belief of ours is that we want to collaborate with the authorities and co-create this future in India. And we have deep engagements and relationships with central government, state government, city governments, everywhere. And, they now see us as a force for good because of the number of livelihoods we generate, because of the congestion that we reduce in the cities, and because of the pollution that we reduce in our cities."

Driver training is another unique operating challenge in India. Many of the drivers that are recruited don't own a car and don't have driver's licenses. To overcome this challenge and be able to boast 800,000 drivers and 700,000 vehicles, Ola runs 15 centres around the country to give recruits residential training for a month in driving, car maintenance, customer service, financial literacy, and even yoga.

But all that effort has not always been met with gratitude, particularly when drivers had their takings reduced by both Ola and Uber. In early 2017, a series of protests by drivers across India were staged to express their displeasure over the reduction of driver incentives by the two companies. Ola and Uber held their ground and drivers returned to work realising that they would be at the losing end if they continued to demonstrate.

Ola has not been travelling on a smooth road when it comes to management recruitment either. Both its Chief Financial Officer and Chief Marketing Officer left after a year with the company and both at about the same time. On what went wrong, Aggarwal had this to offer: "What we realised is that the entrepreneurial nature is a key for senior management. Working at a startup, you need to work without dogma, you need to be able to get your hands dirty, and really look at a problem in its face and peel it layer by layer. It's not just a work environment of managing the ship, because the ship is not there!"

And what about *his* role as founder and CEO? Does a founder have too much at stake to make good, dispassionate decisions as a professional CEO? Unsurprisingly, Aggarwal believes that he is able to handle both well enough. "The best companies in the world are where the founders scale up to do both. And, if you look at most global companies in the internet and technology space, the founders have led these companies as professional CEOs also because these are very fast changing environments, and you need the entrepreneurial passion that a founder would dream, along with the execution machine that a professional would set up. And, it's best that the two end up being the same thing."

Paranoia

The similarities between Ola and Grab have extended to both companies moving into the payments space. Ola Money was launched in late 2015 and one a half years later, Aggarwal reported profitability, with Ola being "the second or third largest wallet" in volume. Where Ola Money used to be limited to paying for rides on the Ola platform, it can now be used to pay for groceries, hotels, and flights. India is expected to see US$700 billion in digital transactions by 2022, with 80% of the urban population going cashless.[8]

> Are we growing fast enough? Are we doing things fast enough? Are we learning fast enough? The question is always fast.

While the digital wallet landscape in India grows, Southeast Asia is a laggard in comparison. Cash is still king in countries like Indonesia and the Philippines. Even in Singapore, which is the leading technology hub in the region, only 4% of transactions are made through new payment methods.[9] But observers agree that it is a matter of time before the take up rate gains momentum, particularly as regulators are working to streamline the system.

To get a head start, Grab extended its digital wallet in late 2017 beyond payment for its rides to enabling users to purchase food and beverage in some outlets in Singapore. A rollout is expected in the coming months to the rest of Southeast Asia pending regulatory approvals. And plans in that area are big. Not only did the company nab the engineering head of India's largest wallet, Paytm, it also announced that US$2.5 billion will be pumped into the payments business.[10]

For all the early successes and the meteoric rise of Grab and Ola, the two millennial founders remain grounded — out of necessity. Being in the technology space, tomorrow may be too late. The plethora of solutions and possibilities has never been more readily available, while the threat of being too slow constantly hovers. "Everyone is coming up with innovative, new, different approaches to solving similar problems," said Tan. "To us, what matters is focus. We know what we're trying to solve, we're focused and prioritising it, and we're bringing the best talent in possible to do it as quickly as possible," she said.

To keep up with the breakneck speed in the industry, Tan is incessant in her self-talk. "Are we growing fast enough? Are we doing things fast enough? Are we learning fast enough? The question is always fast, because we know we are doing things. Are we doing the right things in the most efficient manner, ultimately leading you to the fastest path? That's the same set of questions I ask no matter what we do."

Complacency is, therefore, not even in her vocabulary. "It's difficult to be. I wake up everyday thinking about what else we should be doing and can be doing. I think it's something that drives us, especially Anthony, myself, and the rest of our management team. It's in our personalities, it's in our DNA. We know that there's so much more that we can do and therefore every single day we wake up wanting to do it. I think it's going to be a long time before we get complacent," she said, before adding, "And the day that we are, please kick us, because we're not doing our jobs."

Aggarwal shares the same compulsion to keep innovating, particularly since solutions are not copyright. Innovation therefore has to be "about taking an early leap." Doing new things is par for the course. "One of the core cultural traits of Ola is we are a very experimental company. We have many firsts, globally, and we never shy away from an experiment that fails. We believe that it's good to fail early and take learnings from that, and then, in the future, apply those learnings in a different context," said Aggarwal, referring to Ola's food delivery service which was shut down a year after it was launched. At the same time, Ola has had several successful firsts — the first ride-sharing company to own their own fleet of cars and the first to include the ubiquitous Indian auto rickshaw taxi on its app, the latter being the company's fastest growing business today, according to Aggarwal.

And the work has only just begun. "Our mission is to build mobility for a billion Indians. And today, we serve only about one or two percent of the population. So, then we have a 100 times to go."

For this rapid-fire entrepreneur, who makes it a point to keep his meetings to a maximum of 30 minutes, work and life is about harmony, not a balance — a peaceful coexistence of tasks and responsibilities interwoven seamlessly. Where there are no distinctions, there is no tedium associated with work. "This is not a job," Aggarwal declared, "I'm living my dream and I hope to live my dream as long as I can."

Notes

1 "Ola eyes profits by FY19; SoftBank reaffirms commitment", The Economic Times, 23 November 2017, <https://economictimes.indiatimes.com/small-biz/startups/newsbuzz/ola-eyes-profits-by-fy19-softbank-reaffirms-commitment/articleshow/61756338.cms >

2 http://www.together-eu.org/docs/83/TOGETHER_Energy_saving_5_Handout_09.pdf

3 Palan Balakrishnan, "Auto industry must change gears now", 14 November 2017, The Hindu Business Line, <http://www.thehindubusinessline.com/opinion/auto-industry-must-change-gears-now/article9960390.ece>

4 Rajan Anandan, Rohit Sipahimalani, Alap Bharadwaj, Jaideep Jhangiani, Danny Kim, Soumi Ramesh, "e-conomy SEA: Unlocking the $200B Digital Opportunity", 27 May 2016, Think with Google, <http://apac.thinkwithgoogle.com/research-studies/e-conomy-sea-unlocking-200b-digital-opportunity.html>

5 Anirban Sen, "Uber looks to step up India investments", Livemint, 28 November 2017, <http://www.livemint.com/Companies/qITIgZHFNNR7mQTIcBdPRI/Uber-looks-to-step-up-India-investments.html>

6 Sunny Sen, "Uber India in top gear, set to invest another $1 billion soon", Hindustan Times, 16 August 2016.

7 "80% of Uber, Ola cabs don't have permits to ply in Delhi, says minister", The Indian Express, 19 June 2015.

8 "India Digital Payment Systems Market Worth $700 billion by 2022 — Industry Research Report at OrbisResearch.com", Reuters, 13 July 2017, <https://www.reuters.com/brand features/venture-capital/article?id=12775>

9 "Growing demand for mobile payment services across Asia", The Straits Times, 19 March 2017 <http://www.straitstimes.com/asia/growing-demand-for-mobile-payment-services-across-asia>

10 Roy Choudhury, "Uber rival Grab says you can now pay restaurant bills using its mobile wallet", CNBC, 1 November 2017, <https://www.cnbc.com/2017/11/01/grab-says-users-can-now-pay-for-goods-using-grabpay.html>

Chapter 14

Taking Indians around the World

Deep Kalra
MakeMyTrip, India

O ne setback fuelled the determination of one man who would not let his pioneering mission to build an online travel agency in India tank. And this despite the convergence of world events that seemed set on taking him down a second time.

For Deep Kalra, the founder of MakeMyTrip, one failure was one too many.

When I met Kalra in 2015 at the Trident Hotel in Gurugram, Haryana, the then 45-year-old slipped through the entrance of the grand hotel mostly unnoticed. There was no entourage. Nothing to distinguish him in his grooming, with a plain open-necked shirt and khakis, although you would notice his six-foot frame and wide smile.

This man's unassuming demeanour, however, belies the weight he carries in the travel and hotel business in India, indeed in the internet consumer business in this populous country of 1.3 billion. If not for him, the hotel would not have gone through the lengths it did to host us, offering a range of locations we could conduct the interview in and facilitating many of our filming requirements.

And it wasn't even as if he was pulling rank. He seemed pleasantly surprised, even slightly embarrassed, when we told him how easy it was to work with the hotel only because it was him we were talking to.

An inauspicious start

Failure can break or make a person. Kalra's first failure in setting up the American chain of bowling alleys, AMF, was one too many for him. The setback became fuel for him to succeed at his next venture. "I had a failure dot already in my mind graph," he said. "I don't think I wanted another one because two dots make a line."

> I had a failure dot already in my mind graph. I don't think I wanted another one because two dots make a line.

In 2000, Kalra launched an online agency that allowed people, particularly the overseas Indian market, to find the best flights though the internet. But it was to be a turbulent ride for MakeMyTrip from the get-go. A few months after the company's inception, the exhilaration of the dot-com boom, which Kalra had hoped to ride on, went into a tailspin.

Fortunately for Kalra, a US$2 million fund was secured just before things went bust. It was a princely sum back then but it fizzled out soon enough when four planes crashed into various landmarks in the US in 2001, including the World Trade Center in New York. The infamous 9/11 terror attacks brought global air travel to a standstill.

But bad things, as they say, come in threes. A year later, just when people felt safe enough to travel again, severe acute respiratory syndrome, or SARS, the fatal infectious disease, spread across Asia. More than 8,000 people were infected and 774 died from the disease. Yet another blow to an industry that was barely getting on its feet.

"Pretty much everything that could go wrong went wrong," recalled Kalra. But he soldiered on, even through the 18 particularly lean months when he and his management team went without a salary.

What do entrepreneurs like Kalra say to themselves and their teams when circumstances beyond their control toss them around like a leaf in a hurricane? And what's to stop these well-qualified candidates from falling back on a steady pay check as an employee? After all, at the age

Pretty much everything that could go wrong went wrong.

of 30, armed with a good degree and experience as a business development manager at GE Capital, Kalra would have been welcomed at any multinational, ready to take the burden of a struggling startup off him.

Kalra put it down to two factors. The first was the data coming out of the conversion metric — the measurement internet folks use to figure out how far visitors on their site go until they get to the point of sale. It's "the Holy Grail" of the business, according to Kalra. And the data was positive.

But Kalra didn't just rely on that. He looked to the minutest of victories to spur the team on.

"Way back then, we actually measured our business by the hour," said Kalra. "And we would compare an hour on Tuesday, let's say, 1p.m. to 2p.m., with last year's 1p.m. to 2p.m. — leaving out any exceptions like holidays — and say, 'Are we getting better?'" And the answer was positive.

"The other side, which I think is the most important one for any entrepreneur, is the fuzzy one," Kalra revealed, going beyond the statistics. "Because that's the one which you really get from your gut. I mean, you really get, 'Is this going to happen or not?' And I promise you, at that point of time, I felt it was going to happen. I asked two of my senior colleagues, both of which became co-founders later, and they felt the same. So, we really felt we were on to something."

When I suggested that his perseverance was a function of his predisposed optimism, Kalra offered a more pragmatic perspective: "I think I would always look at where's the opportunity here. There's a challenge, but where's the opportunity? Because I think they are two sides of the same coin."

The saving grace for MakeMyTrip in the first five years, was the unique market they served — non-resident Indians in the US. Despite the fear associated with travel, this group of people were still commuting to and from India — not for leisure, but familial obligations. At that time, India had the third largest number of people in the world who lived outside of their home country.

"People weren't coming to holiday in Asia. They were coming back home, visiting friends and relatives. They were bringing their parents to them out there, kids were being born, parents were getting sick, people were dying. So, that need for travel was very different, very inelastic, and that kept going," he explained.

On days when the going got especially tough — and there were many — Kalra would motivate his team by doing something counter-intuitive. Depression Day, or D-Day, was declared one day in a month. On that day, everyone could give in to their dark, discouraged, and pessimistic selves. It was the day to sulk and mope and lament. But once that was over, the next 29 days were all about pushing on and looking up. Happily, D-Day hasn't been declared for a long time since. There's been no need to.

From a small team of 60 people when it started, MakeMyTrip has close to 2,000 employees today. It has seen revenue rising steadily over the years at a compound annual growth rate of 14% over the last five years. Apart of airline tickets, hotel bookings also contribute to its bottomline. In 2010, the company went public on Nasdaq and the company has been acquiring complementary businesses since.

On the macro scale, revenue from online travel sales in India in 2018 is expected to come in at US$5.6 billion while 14% compound annual growth rate between 2018 and 2022 can be anticipated.[1] And MakeMyTrip can proudly claim pole position in market share.

Travel bookings in India are also increasingly being made on mobile devices. Catching the wave early in the game, MakeMyTrip launched its mobile app in 2012 and today half of its domestic hotel bookings and 30% of its domestic flight reservations are made through the app. To encourage the trend, special deals are given to app users only. The demonetisation measures announced in late 2016 to take 85% of cash out of circulation have led to an upsurge in digital payments. Online transactions have also increased.

In 2016, the number of middle-class Indians surpassed the 250 million mark and along with that, travel trends are looking good for the business. "We're seeing frequent trips, weekend getaways, and regional travel. The key markets (regional travel) are Thailand, Singapore, Malaysia, Hong Kong, Dubai, and islands like Mauritius, Maldives, and Sri Lanka. We're finding people travelling much more than they ever did. And I can see this trend moving in one direction," Kalra said, optimistically.

The costs of keeping ahead of the curve

For revenue to remain positive, the cost of keeping ahead of the curve is high. Back in 1965, Intel co-founder Gordon Moore posited that the power of the computer chip doubles every 18 months. This fun fact has come to be known as Moore's Law. For those in the technology space, keeping up with the exponential pace is a matter of survival and disruption is not just a buzzword. For Kalra, it's a race he must keep up with, if not, be ahead. "You're really planning for where the puck is going to be," he said.

The punishing business of technology is real and incessant. "If tomorrow, technology allows you to connect seamlessly to the 40,000 hotels in India without all the connectors that we have, and we're not part of that connectivity, then we've lost out," he said. "Someone's going to eat our lunch."

> You're really planning for where the puck is going to be.

For Kalra, the key to staying ahead, therefore, is acquisitions. Since 2012 the company has been on a buying spree acquiring, on average, about two travel-related companies a year, not just in India, but also in Thailand, Singapore, and the Netherlands. In 2014, Kalra and his partners set aside US$15 million to invest in startups involved in developing technology for the travel industry. The first of the fund's investment was Simplotel, a travel website in India, while part of it went to HolidayIQ, India's answer to TripAdvisor.

Kalra had enthused about the technology and traction in the market, describing the new breed of internet entrepreneurs, or techpreneurs, and their products as "phenomenal," "exciting," and "brilliant." Instead of beating them at their game, he's happy to take them on board, making the way for a consolidation of online travel players.

In 2016, Kalra made his most costly acquisition. MakeMyTrip merged with its rival, South Africa-based Ibibo, taking up a 60% stake in the new entity. The combined worth is valued at US$2 billion. MakeMyTrip issued US$960 million of shares for the acquisition.

The company's investments help explain the company's losses since 2013, despite increasing revenue. Fiscal year 2017 saw net revenue

> The nature of the internet business, particularly B2C, is that once the flip comes, then, you get tremendous economies of scale.

spiking up 62% on the back of its merger with competitor Ibibo, to US$274 million. At the same time, net loss also widened to US$110 million from US$88 million.

Expenses have been channelled towards marketing and promotions and pushing hotel packages — a segment that sees margins four times higher than airline ticketing.[2] In the relentless pursuit of revenue and customer acquisition, cash incentives and loyalty programmes have been dished out in response to increased competition in the domestic travel market in India. With promotions and marketing outpacing revenue in some quarters, analysts have pushed back the company's break-even beyond 2020.[3]

Back in 2015 when we had met, Kalra was unfazed by the company's losses. His focus was on taking a bigger share of the market. "We still believe in the basics of per-unit economics where per-unit, we will never lose money." Unit economics is a common measure used among startups to estimate the long-term value of a customer against the cost of acquiring him.

Kalra's adamant that their marketing efforts will pay off. And once again, the perennial optimist shone through, "The nature of the internet business, particularly B2C, is that once the flip comes, then, you get tremendous economies of scale."

According to serial angel investor Fritz Demopoulos who knows Kalra personally, Kalra "can turn a profit any time if he wanted to." But apparently placating shareholders with short-term gains is not part of Kalra's agenda for the company. And investors seem similarly patient and confident, with an injection of US$330 million in fresh funds in 2017.

Releasing control and refocusing

Kalra has stepped back from the operations of MakeMyTrip India and taken on the role of executive chairman and Group CEO, keeping a lookout for M&As and investments. But he's still mindful that growth must also happen organically. Developers work on about five "critical things" — programmes that can lead to that next breakthrough. He banks on a 20% success rate. Failure is par for the course.

> If you don't try and someone else goes and cracks that code, and actually finds the Holy Grail, then you'll be left far, far behind...

"If you don't try and someone else goes and cracks that code, and actually finds the Holy Grail, then you'll be left far, far behind because catching up is very hard," Kalra said. "People can copy the front-end. But the real magic — I believe the Devil's under the hood, really — is behind the scenes. And you have to figure those technologies out for the future."

It can never be easy for founders to relinquish control of the companies they started, especially those they brought from trough to triumph, as Kalra did with MakeMyTrip. And that's a fact not lost on him. On handing the reins of the local operations to Rajesh Magow, his former CFO and founding team member, Kalra was painfully aware that he could, by instinct, step in to take control. So, he's quick to have himself checked.

"I remind myself all the time that he's running MakeMyTrip India, and I'm not," he said. "I want to give him all the space. And whenever we have these little detailed chats, the first thing I ask him, 'Am I stepping on your shoes? Because, I don't want to. I want you to be the guy in charge and calling the shots.' And I think he's enjoying doing that."

Kalra takes great pleasure in developing people. "I love to give the latitude and it's great fun to see your own colleagues you've worked with, actually grow to become, you know, leaders in every right. It's also, by the way, very, very satisfying." He admitted that benefits come with releasing control, which is "to be away on holiday, and not to have to work."

The focus the company places on people and creating a positive work culture has consistently earned it a spot in the Best Place to Work lists in India.

While Kalra, on paper at least, appears to have handed the reins of control over to his CEO, he remains firmly in the driver's seat overseeing the mergers and acquisitions that have come to be an integral part of this young company's growth. If it isn't about getting over the struggle of the early years, or growing the company through high-profile acquisitions, then MakeMyTrip is constantly jostling for pole position in a business that is intensely competitive. Definitely not a task for the faint-hearted and Kalra, with his eternal optimism and clarity of vision, is proving to be the man for the job.

Notes

1   "Online travel booking: India", The Statistics Portal, <https://www.statista.com/outlook/262/119/online-travel-booking/india#market-arpu>

2   Sunny Sen, "Makemytrip losses to go up in next 2 years", *Financial Express*, 26 October 2015, http://www.financialexpress.com/industry/makemytrip-losses-to-go-up-in-next-2-years/156673/.

3   Biswarup Gooptu, Taslima Khan, "MakeMyTrip-Ibibo merger: How combined entity continues to struggle with problems old and new", Economic Times, 26 January 2018, <https://economictimes.indiatimes.com/small-biz/startups/features/makemytrip-ibibo-merger-how-combined-entity-continues-to-struggle-with-problems-old-and-new/articleshow/62658501.cms>

Chapter 15

Union by Algorithms

Anupam Mittal
People Group, India

T he extent the internet has pervaded our lives cannot be more
intimately witnessed than in the brainchild of Indian internet
entrepreneur, Anupam Mittal. Shaadi.com claims to be the
number one matrimonial website in the world, having brought together
four million people in matrimony.

Mittal stumbled on the radical idea of taking the time-honoured
and venerated Indian tradition of arranged marriages the way of the
internet when he himself was the target of a matchmaker. His parents
had appointed one to be on the lookout for their son while he was a
student in Boston College in 1996. However, instead of the matchmaker
enquiring of his prospective groom, the former became the subject of
Mittal's insatiable curiosity.

"He came and saw me and I actually got very intrigued by what
he did," Mittal recalled. "And I asked him how he went about his
business. And he said he carried around fifty to sixty biodatas in his
bag. And he visited maybe a hundred families which were part of his
personal network. I thought that was very intriguing that the choice
of my life partner was going to be limited by the weight that this man
could carry in his bag and his social reach."

The meeting amounted to nothing for the matchmaker but for the "accidental entrepreneur," as Mittal called himself, it led to a germ of an idea.

"Why not take all these resumes for him, put them on the internet, and do away with all these special limitations and geographical boundaries? And that's kind of what we did. I suggested to him and said, 'Look forget about finding me a match but I've got a business model for you,'" Mittal said, turning the tables on the matchmaker. "I never saw him again but Shaadi was born and that was the start of the journey."

Today, Mittal's People Group not only has Shaadi under its belt but also mobile media service Mauj.com which claims 20 million unique views each month. In 2015, the group sold its other runaway success, Makaan.com, a property search website to PropTiger, a NewsCorp-backed competitor for an undisclosed sum.

On the day of the interview in 2014, Mittal was welcoming and spruced up in a Nehru suit, consistent with the debonair image the then 42-year-old always cuts. He spoke confidently. Unhurried. A savvy spokesman, for sure, as he prefaced his responses with compliments on the "good questions" that were coming his way.

But this slickness was not always a part of his persona. Mittal revealed that he was almost embarrassed by the responses he got when Shaadi first began.

> Nobody took us seriously. It was almost laughable.

"Nobody took us seriously," Mittal recalled. "It was almost laughable. The reactions were very funny sometimes. Disbelief!" The responses were so incredulous that he kept the idea to himself, to steer clear of the negativity.

In India, marriage is a sacred union that involves not just the couple, but the families and the perpetuation of social structures. It is not an affair that two young people should undertake without the involvement of the clan.

Matchmakers play an integral role in bringing families together and to ensure the correct match. These introducers are often relatives themselves. They act as go-betweens to scout for suitable partners and negotiate the arrangements. Factors such as family backgrounds, educational levels of the couple, and value of the dowry are considered during the survey.

Mittal made sure to keep his day job after launching Shaadi. He worked in the US as a product manager in an IT company after graduating. But when the dot-com crash hit at the turn of the millennium, Mittal found himself twiddling his thumbs for a lack of anything productive to do.

By that time, Shaadi had gained enough traction to convince its developer to jump in with both feet. So, with the push of the circumstances in the US and the pull of the increasing popularity of Shaadi, it seemed opportune for Mittal to return to India to "give this baby some legs."

Since Shaadi's launch, many other rivals have jumped on the bandwagon. And while some have gone public, Mittal has held on to his brand which continues to play a dominant role in the industry. Estimates put the growth of the matchmaking business at 14% year on year reaching US$12 million in 2017.[1]

Before the tipping point, however, and as the forerunner of online matrimonial platforms, Mittal's approach was unsurprisingly tentative. In fact, he was caught off guard when the service took off the way it did. "I did expect it to grow. I did think it was a unique and large opportunity but I hadn't, at that time, imagined that we would grow so fast in this business and that people would accept something that went against the very culture and tradition so quickly," he said.

Coding love

In a lot of ways, we're changing the trajectory of humankind.

The novelty of the business concept aside, Mittal and his team take their jobs very seriously. "In a lot of ways, we're changing the trajectory of humankind. And that's the kind of seriousness with which we should take our jobs," he declared unabashedly.

Twenty years into the business, Mittal seems to have it down pat. "When it comes to finding a match you start out very rationally and logically but at some point chemistry kicks in. So, you might end up liking somebody who's exactly the opposite of what you started out defining you like for yourself. So how do you start to understand these nuances of human beings? How do you code that into technology so that technology starts to understand all that?"

"If you brought human beings into the equation of matchmaking," Mittal said, "they will always bring their biases into play in terms of the type of person you may be the most compatible with. But with technology there is no such thing. We can look at what people say, what they do, and how that translates into other people who are like them."

Even Mittal admits that it can all seem out of this world. "It's almost eerie. When you tell us the first few things about yourself, we're pretty much able to, in real time, figure out what kind of person you're looking for."

> We believe that we can use technology to understand human beings and what they're looking for much better than a human being can...

Then, without any guile or hubris, Mittal declared, "We believe that we can use technology to understand human beings and what they're looking for much better than a human being can because of inherent biases."

Mittal claims that with the same technology they can also weed out fake profiles. "We can figure out why you're on the site based on several things — based on the speed with which you type, based on the kind of data that you put in, based on the mismatch between certain data points, based on your activity levels, how you get in touch, how you respond to them. We're able to figure out a lot of things in real time," he said.

The reality of artificial intelligence would all be bound into a perfect fairy tale if the virtual matchmaker had himself found his perfect match in cyberspace. But it was not to be. Instead Mittal met his future wife, model Anchal Kumar, in 2013 through, of all things, mutual friends!

Traversing India's business mine fields

Parents are a vital part of the process in any arranged marriage in India. And most would be unfamiliar with technology, much less searching for the right match over the internet. So, to meet its customers where they are, Shaadi pursued an O2O, or online-to-offline, business model, setting up brick-and-mortar touchpoints throughout India. To make it even more accessible, these outlets are notably located near train stations.

I visited an outlet in Mumbai and found a handful of employees whose duties included talking to customers over the phone and taking walk-in customers through an otherwise perplexing process in front of the desktops. Modern-day matchmakers, not with the traditional connections, but the internet ones.

This nifty business model hinges on technology while riding on the physical presence of stores to overcome the unique challenges India presents. The issue isn't just about the competence of navigating through online transactions among an older generation, but also of infrastructure. While the country boasts one of the largest internet penetration rates in the world, with 450 million in 2017 to an estimate of 600 million by 2020, it still has one of the slowest speeds at 3.5 Mbps against a global average of 6.4 Mbps.[2]

Then there's the issue of payments. End 2016 saw an upheaval in India's banking system as Prime Minister Narendra Modi scrapped the two largest-denominated notes in circulation, or 85% of cash in the system. While digital payments have soared, cash, however, has not lost its place in the economy. In fact, it's been reported that while the value of cash withdrawals from ATMs have declined since demonetisation, the number of transactions have actually increased.[3]

In 2013 when I met with Mittal, he revealed that 50% of their payments in India come from people paying cash at their homes. "We actually have somebody who visits their home to collect the cash to activate their membership. So, look, necessity is, as they say, the mother of invention," he said matter-of-factly. Cash is still king in India, particularly in the rural areas. Indeed, much of the informal economy in India still transacts in cash, as do many of Shaadi's older customers.

India is a challenging place to do business, whether you're a foreigner or a local. There are the layers of bureaucracy, the resulting delays in completion of work, and the usual complaints of patchy infrastructure, utilities, and obscure and disparate regulations. Rising above the vicissitudes inherent in the environment necessitates remarkable inventiveness and resilience. It isn't just about who you know, but *how* you get over the many hurdles along the way. In fact, this can-do spirit is captured aptly in Hindi — *jugaad*. It's an oft-uttered colloquialism used when things don't go as planned. Unlike resignation, *jugaad*

> If you don't believe in God, come spend some time in India.

suggests an acceptance of things gone wrong and a readiness to find a hack.

Mittal expresses it well and with truthful candour, explaining how he operates an internet company in a country with patchy internet connections. "One of the things I often say is, if you don't believe in God, come spend some time in India," he said. "Things just seem to fall in place here somehow. So is the case with the internet."

"People have no problems waiting," he continued. "People have no problems with dropped connections. People don't care about logging in over and over again. They just seem to get by. From a Western perspective, especially when I moved back from the US, we take things for granted. You're so used to having your internet speed at a certain level. You're so used *not* having to log in over and over again. That gets really frustrating as soon as something is even a little out of the ordinary. Same is the case for the roads, infrastructure, or the public transport system working a certain way, or water and electricity — everything that you take for granted in Western cities. In India, we just manage to get by with whatever little that we have."

The next threshold

While resourcefulness and resilience are important traits to possess, one that has eluded the Indians on the path towards the knowledge economy is creativity. IT professionals, one of India's best exports, have not demonstrated enough innovative thinking — a bone of contention for Mittal.

> We love to get paid and build for others as opposed to trying to come up with novel ideas that could change the world.

He distinguished the doers from the creators, finding the latter lacking in India. "The real new world industries or innovation industries are only about 10–15 years old in this country. So, you don't really have the talent or the academic institutions that foster innovation and creativity. We are too much of a 'me-too' type of mindset. We're too much of a service-led model where we play it safe. And caution is what we use to build business models and we love to get paid and build for others as opposed to trying to come up with novel ideas that could change the world."

"IT consultants go after applied problems. They go after solutions to very specific problems. That does take some level of creativity. It takes some rational and logical thinking but it doesn't take innovation *per se*," said Mittal. Then zooming in on the rub, he remarked, "When we're talking about innovation, I think of innovation that can change the way we do things. I think of Apple, I think of a model like Shaadi. I think of something that completely changes the trajectory of how you were doing something. So, there's a before and after."

Some time after my interview with Mittal, India's IT czar, Narayana Murthy, founder of one of India's earliest and largest technology companies, Infosys, echoed the sentiment. He declared that there hadn't been one "earthshaking" invention in the country in the last 60 years.[4] Research, he said, has not led to anything that would raise a global household name from India. Murthy bemoaned the insularity within the institutions of learning and called for more interactions with foreign universities and students.

> The internet ensures that the knowledge that's available to somebody in the [Silicon] Valley is also available to an engineer in India, if he so seeks it out.

However, that's not to say that Murthy has thrown in the towel and given up on ever seeing innovation hit the shores of India. Both Mittal and Murthy are active angel investors constantly on the lookout for bright sparks.

Though still lagging behind China, the start-up scene is heating up in India with 10 unicorns raised so far. These are new technology companies that are valued at more than US$1 billion each. And if one is judged by how much money one puts where one's mouth is, then Mittal is talking lakhs and crores of rupees. He is one of the most active angel investors in India, with over 50 investments. These include successes such as Ola and Little Eye Labs (the latter was eventually acquired by Facebook).

Mittal was hopeful and had even declared this "the decade of entrepreneurship" in India with a generation that's reaping the fruit of their parents' hard work. Uninhibited by the fear of poverty and enlightened by access to information and funding, India's new generation of workers are opting to go out on a limb to chart their own courses. In a country of 1.3 billion people and the median age of

29 years by 2020, the youngest population in the world,[5] the intensity of the competition can only produce the most resilient entrepreneurs with the brightest ideas.

"I'm very enthused by the new crop of entrepreneurs. And I meet these people almost on a weekly basis. These are kids in their 20s and they don't have this hang up that maybe our generation did in that we have to be a little more cautious and, really, they haven't seen scarcity in their lives," Mittal pointed out. "They are children of a different generation. And they're thinking global; they're thinking disruption; they're thinking innovation. Today, fortunately, the internet ensures that the knowledge that's available to somebody in the [Silicon] Valley is also available to an engineer in India, if he so seeks it out."

The frenzy of activity in the internet scene demands an all-or-nothing approach. With Mittal's input and the irrepressible energy of the young turks looking to build that next unicorn, it'll be a promising future for startups in India. In a land of contrasts, where many roads lead to one destination, with as many bends along the way, it will be the *jugaad* spirit that will hold out for the next big thing out of India.

Notes

1 Bhumika Khatri, "Matchmaking Portal Matrimony Clocks $13.06 Mn Revenue In Its Last Quarter", Inc42, 1 February 2018, <https://inc42.com/buzz/matchmaking-matrimony-revenue/>

2 Ivan Mehta, "India's Average Internet Speed Is 3.5 Mbps", Huffpost, 1 July 2016, <http://www.huffingtonpost.in/2016/07/01/india_n_10764914.html>

3 AP Hota, "Why ATMS will not go extinct anytime soon in India", The Economic Times, 2 July 2017, <https://economictimes.indiatimes.com/industry/banking/finance/banking/50-years-after-invention-atms-are-still-here-to-stay/articleshow/59403164.cms>

4 "No earth-shaking Indian invention in 60 years: N R Narayana Murthy", The Times of India, 16 July 2015, <http://www.rediff.com/business/report/no-invention-earth-shaking-idea-from-india-in-60-years-murthy/20150715.htm>

5 Girija Shivakumar, "India is set to become the youngest country by 2020", The Hindu, 17 April 2013, <http://www.thehindu.com/news/national/india-is-set-to-become-the-youngest-country-by-2020/article4624347.ece>

Part VI

CRISIS MANAGEMENT

I't's often said that the true mettle of a leader is tested not in the best, but in the worst of times. Leaders who demonstrate masterclass abilities in managing a company through growth may be rendered paralysed in moments of crisis.

Crisis management and communication training programmes are foundational for all top management personnel in large corporations. We've witnessed giants of industries crumble from the failure to manage crises well. BP's Deepwater Horizon oil spill is the classic case study of what *not* to do in a crisis with the focus on CEO Tony Hayward's petulant handling of the disaster ("I'd like my life back" was his famed retort to the massive clean-up that followed); while Johnson & Johnson's swift and open response to the Tylenol poisoning incident is held up as exemplary despite the fact that its cyanide-laced painkillers killed seven in Chicago in 1982. In this age of social media, where the scrutiny that companies are under is so intense, the hard truth that everything rises and falls on leadership is ever more pronounced.

One event in recent years has bound the fates of many around the world and given rise to stories of survival and utter collapse. The Global Financial Crisis (GFC) of 2008, precipitated by the shut down of one of the oldest financial institutions on Wall Street, brought home the stark reality of the interdependence of the world economy once again.

In the early 2000s, banks in the US, in order to boost their loan portfolio, began giving out loans to borrowers who had patchy credit histories. Lehman Brothers, one of the biggest investment banks, bought up some of these subprime loans. For the immediate few years after the acquisitions, these investments made good money for the bank, as households took up high-interest loans, using their mortgages as security. But the illusory party had to end when interest rates were raised and housing prices fell in 2006. Homeowners defaulted on their loans and soon a convergence of events precipitated the GFC. The bank could not bear under the weight of hefty defaults in subprime mortgages and its high leverage and had to declare the largest bankruptcy in history, with US$619 billion in debt.

With the world's largest economy slumped, trade slowed down and China's once-bustling factories languished. Confidence around the world began to be shaken right down to the petty trader in Hyderabad in India and the mom-and-pop investor in Singapore.

To helm an organisation tossed about by circumstances not of its own making, a leader can either hold tight and ride out the storm, or shore up the strengths of the organisation and hope that'll keep the ship afloat. There is no source to turn to to stem the bleeding. It is, instead, an invisible hand wrecking visible losses — an unseen enemy.

Two of my guests shared their experiences heading their banks in India and Singapore during the GFC. In both instances, panic struck their retail customers on word of Lehman's collapse. In one instance the impact was massive but short-lived. In the other, it involved a small group of customers but wrecked havoc on the bank's reputation and raised legal and even moral issues.

Attempts to compare the two leaders' handling of the crisis would be baseless since the circumstances were vastly different. However, the insights into their strategies in dealing with the drama that played out will reveal pragmatism and level-headedness, even in the face of unpopular measures.

Chapter 16

Calm Amid the Storm

Chanda Kochhar
ICICI Bank, India

C handa Kochhar was a picture of poise. Elegantly bejewelled, she carried her slight frame, wrapped in a sari, with a determined gait. She wore a professional smile that seemed to say, "Hello, pleased to meet you. Let's get going."

It's something you would expect from the head of India's leading private bank, ICICI, an entity with consolidated assets of US$153 billion in 2017. A 30-year veteran of the bank, she climbed the ranks from the position of management trainee. In fact, she credits her ability to pre-empt situations, a vital leadership quality, in her view, not just to having done her time at different business units in the bank but growing some of them from inception.

The advantage of insight is invaluable. "I think in that sense, I feel that I kind of understand this organisation from every which way. And that gives me that added ability to be able to say things," she maintained.

The accolades, awards and acknowledgement this veteran banker has received over the years are dutifully archived by staff. PR collateral includes *Forbes* and *Fortune* magazines' 'Most Powerful Women in the World' several years running, *Bloomberg Markets* 'Most Influential

People in Global Finance' as well as several other shout-outs from local and government organisations.

Kochhar's steady rise to the top is a classic rags-to-riches tale of a bright young girl brought up by a single mother after her father passed away when she was 13. A star student, she found her place in ICICI upon graduation and soon caught the attention of long-time CEO K.V. Kamath, who took her under his wing and mentored her.

> In today's scenario, you cannot make a long-term plan for one year and then sit back and say we will just implement that plan.

When I met Kochhar in 2013, the Indian economy was in a tailspin. In 2010, GDP was hovering at 10% but the euphoria didn't last long, as the figure slid rapidly to 6% a year later and 5% in 2013. The uncertainty at that time was further spooked by talk of the US Federal Reserve's unwinding of its Quantitative Easing measures, which sent foreign investors ditching the rupee, precipitating capital outflows. To stem the slide, which saw the rupee fall against the US dollar by 20% in three months, the central bank tightened monetary policy, making bank borrowings more expensive. ICICI, as the largest private lender, was not spared the gloom. From May to August that year, its share price slid 30% as investors also worried about the spike in bad loans.

Amid the uncertainty, the managing director maintained the old adage that the only constant in life is change, or in her case, volatility. Survival for any organisation is about being dynamic. Even her speech pattern that gushed fluidly from one thought to the next, sidestepping the need for punctuation, mirrored the constant flux that she operated in.

"In today's scenario, you cannot make a long-term plan for one year and then sit back and say we will just implement that plan," Kochhar rationalised. "So, the recognition is that there is volatility in the environment and, therefore, you have to always steer the organisation all the time and continue to do that and not get flustered by it, I think that's very important."

That ability to stay calm and unfazed by buffeting waves provides a glimpse of the tenacity that has enabled Kochhar to helm the bank through good and bad times since 2007 as joint managing director, before going solo in 2009.

"The leader's ability has to be to absorb a lot of this stress of volatility and not allow that stress to be passed on to the team. And allow the team to continue to focus on execution and so be mentally prepared that you'll have to continue to face volatility, keep the organisation ready for the next volatility, be ready to change course as and when required. And through all this, maintain your calm and cool." If her rapid-fire commentary on how she manages under constant variables in the Indian banking system already sounds heightened, one can only imagine how consuming the task is in practice.

But it is her uncanny ability to maintain an apparent equanimity that has helped her ride the tumultuous waves of crises that have hit the bank — one of which had taken place just before we met.

In 2013, a reporter had gone undercover posing as an interested party in a possible money-laundering attempt. He had recorded a conversation with ICICI employees who suggested there were many ways illegal money could be transferred through the bank. One way was to accept black money and invest it in insurance products and even provide lockers for the cash to be stashed away.[1]

The exposé that named three banks caused a stir and an immediate response from them to investigate. Two days after the revelation, ICICI suspended 18 employees from the bank for further investigation.

> The leader's ability has to be to absorb a lot of this stress of volatility and not allow that stress to be passed on to the team.

Kochhar admitted to being caught unawares when she first received word of the allegations. "I think the entire way in which the allegations were put forth and projected, I think that definitely took me by surprise." But only momentarily.

"It comes back to saying, 'Well the fact is that it has hit you, so what do you need to do to handle the situation?'"

The first option was to hold an internal inquiry, putting together a list of audit companies to look into the matter while attending to the regulator's questions. Then, it was time to look into the bank's processes and systems squarely and ask questions about them. "We should have no qualms in saying we need to continue to improve," she pointed out.

Still, it was the robustness of the bank's frameworks that Kochhar fell back on. "We had this basic conviction to say that, broadly, our processes and systems are strong," she asserted.

As it turned out, the three banks were fined by the central bank, with ICICI footing INR10 million (US$146,000) — a slap on the wrist. The move by the regulator was seen by many as an appeasement to the international financial community and symbolic of the country's stance against money laundering.[2]

> We should have no qualms in saying we need to continue to improve.

Weathering this incident, however, was not anywhere as disquieting as the one that hit the bank during the 2008 Global Financial Crisis. Though it lasted a few days, that crisis has been etched in Chanda Kochhar's memory for a lifetime. And her legacy as a banker.

ICICI bank run

In 2008, the impossible happened. A venerable financial institution with a 150-year history collapsed. Lehman Brothers, a US-based behemoth with more than US$600 billion in assets, crumbled against massive losses from the subprime crisis in the US. It earned the unenviable reputation of being the company that filed the largest bankruptcy ever, with a US$619 billion debt. The collapse of the bank had a domino effect on other financial institutions around the world that had invested in its products and resulted in massive losses for themselves and their customers.

One of these banks was ICICI, which had US$80 million in exposure to Lehman, much of which was written down. By most accounts that was a small amount compared to what many other banks had lost. But it was the culmination of various events that triggered panic among its customers.

The fear of other bankruptcies in the US and Europe and ICICI's exposure to foreign banks sent jitters throughout India. The bank's bad loans and astoundingly high level of unsecured loans at 55% stoked the trepidation further.[3] The fact that ICICI had US$105 billion in consolidated assets and a higher than required capital adequacy ratio was of little assurance to its customers.

With sentiment prevailing over technical indicators, snaking queues formed at the bank and ATMs. The country's central bank stepped in to assure borrowers that there was more than enough liquidity in the bank. It even offered to shore it up in the unlikely event that the bank could not meet demand.

Kochhar was joint MD at the time and was being groomed to take over from K.V. Kamath who'd been at the helm since 1996. Her take on the situation was clear — it was the crisis of perception. After all, losses from Lehman amounted to about 0.1% of the bank's assets. But rationale would not prevail over sentiment, try as she did to pacify customers and investors.

"I made sure that we communicated with every segment, whether it was the most matured investor or analyst, or it was the smallest customer who was not even aware of the global financial crisis and the nuances around it," she recalled.

> If you shut the branch and go away, that takes away their confidence.

It was the action that she put to the words that really quelled the storm after a stressful few days. Her directive to her staff — keep the branches open for 24 hours and dispatch truckloads of cash to fill up ATMs around the country. And if one ATM had run out, a bus would be chartered to bring customers to another one nearby.

"Let everybody come in, explain to them what the situation is, but still if they want their money, give it to them," was her instruction to her staff. "When you give (customers) the money, they get the confidence. If you shut the branch and go away, that takes away their confidence. It was a few harrowing days."

Through the crisis, Kochhar kept her head above the water and refused to be inundated by doubts. She was sure of the bank's financial viability even when others were not. Her strategy in dealing with the crisis was to assess its scale and deal head-on with the immediate challenges.

"The way I looked at the size of the challenge was not to say that the bank can go bankrupt, but I think the size of the challenge indeed was that we had to plan for huge amounts of cash being available at every branch, at every ATM. So, in that sense, it was a large-scale problem," explained Kochhar.

"We, in fact, in our minds calculated that if everybody continuously kept withdrawing from all our ATMs, how much cash will we need to keep available to give out. And we moved a few thousands of crore of cash all over India to keep our branches and ATMs full of cash. So, in that sense, we recognized that the size of the problem was huge. We did not underprepare ourselves for it. But, at the same time, I think I had that broad confidence that we were financially viable. We were financially stable, and we needed to do everything to maintain and retain that stability, and go through this period."

Within days, calm finally prevailed. Confidence, however, continued to waver in the bank's share price until months later. The *annus horribilis* of the Global Financial Crisis shaved off 80% of ICICI's market capitalisation from an all-time high at the beginning of the year. It was only in March the following year that its share price began to recover.

***

> When I get home, I'm a wife, I'm a mother, I'm a housekeeper, I'm a daughter, I'm a daughter-in-law...

In 2016, Kochhar wrote a letter to her daughter which went viral on social media. It was a heartfelt message from a mother to a daughter about succeeding in life with the support of family. In it, she referred to the episode of the 2008 bank run and revealed how she took time off during the crisis to watch her son play at a squash tournament.

Nothing she said in her letter surprised me or was out of character from the person I met three years earlier. The obvious importance she places on family is a consistent narrative weaved through her life.

Back when we met, Kochhar was known to clock out of work by 6 p.m., which was not to say she wasn't on her devices until midnight some days. "I don't think it's possible to say at this cut-off time, office is out and home is in," she insisted. "I think the ability has to be to say that whatever requires attention gets it. And one attention doesn't come at the cost of the other. So, that's why I feel it all has to be just bound together."

Ask this woman who's been named consistently one of the world's most powerful women what her simple pleasures are and she readily tells you it's being able to spend time with family.

"When I get home, I'm a wife, I'm a mother, I'm a housekeeper, I'm a daughter, I'm a daughter-in-law — I'm everything! But, believe me, I enjoy each one of those roles," Kochhar happily declared. "Nobody's forcing me to do it and if I'm doing it out of my own choice, it's only me who can be responsible for doing it well. And even if that's a little bit of hard work, I enjoy doing it and I feel privileged that I'm able to do all that."

Kochhar's ability to merge realms that others separate and the fluidity that she moves from one task to another and one issue to the next must all contribute to her sensibility in uncertainty. Indeed, she must remain unflappable and level-headed, if she is to run India's largest private bank in an environment where volatility is the order of every day.

Notes

1 "Money-laundering by big banks, alleges Cobrapost; banks deny charges", NDTV, 14 March 2013, <http://www.ndtv.com/india-news/money-laundering-by-big-banks-alleges-cobrapost-banks-deny-charges-516170>

2 Between 2016 and 2017, India went down 10 places to 88 out of 146 countries in the Basel Anti-Money-Laundering Index, indicating significant improvement in the country's robustness in dealing with the scourge.

3 MC Govardhana Rangan & Anita Bhoir, "How Chanda Kochhar saved ICICI Bank from being engulfed by Lehman bankruptcy", Economic Times, 18 September 2013, <//economic-times.indiatimes.com/articleshow/22678026.cms?intenttarget=no&utm_source=contentof-interest&utm_medium=text&utm_campaign=cppst>

Chapter 17

From Regional Epidemic to Global Crisis

Koh Boon Hwee

Development Bank of Singapore and Singapore Airlines, Singapore

When a man has either chaired or sat on the boards of organisations of Singapore Inc., in some cases for over 15 years, you can only guess at the depth and breadth of his experience. Why guess if I could meet him personally and tap on his insights and make him a guest on the show?

By the time I had met him, Koh Boon Hwee was 65 and had stepped back from the role of chairman at three of Singapore's largest companies: SingTel, Singapore Airlines (SIA), and Development Bank of Singapore (DBS), to something less stressful — relatively. He has since founded Credence Partners, a venture capital firm, with two others, that manages a S$200 million fund — a drop in the ocean compared to the billion-dollar organisations that he used to oversee. Credence invests in small- and medium-sized enterprises (SMEs) in Southeast Asia, in particular in the high-tech and IT sectors.

Koh still chairs the boards of various companies under Singapore's largest private property developer Far East Organization and Nanyang Technological University's board of trustees and gives advice as a director of US-based Agilent Technologies as well as Singapore's sovereign wealth fund, GIC — duties that keep him busy, albeit at a much less rigorous pace than before. Along the way, he keeps an eye out for promising startups and gives them a leg-up as an angel investor.

Koh expressed surprise that we would even invite him on the show, self-effacingly wondering who would even want to listen to him. Modesty aside, he has much to show for having guided two of the companies he chaired through some of their most turbulent times, proving that humility and trials go hand in glove.

Koh was the golden child of academia — a graduate of Imperial College London (First Class Honours) and Harvard Business School (MBA, Distinction). Studies came easy for him. Even before his A-level results were out, the precocious teenager had already made his mark in the corporate world, disguised as a computer card puncher.

Koh had taken up the temporary position in the IT consultancy business of Ernst & Young. In two weeks, he was the fastest at the job. But the mindlessness of the task compelled him to approach the head of the business for another position. He asked to do "what those other guys are doing," pointing to the programmers.

Looking back, Koh explained his audacity plainly. While others may have been intimidated and discouraged by the high likelihood of rejection from the boss, he was rational about it: To a tee. "The downside is, he can say no, and then I'm exactly where I was before — punching cards."

But it wasn't a no. Instead, Koh was handed three books on programming to read over the weekend. Young Koh turned up for work on Monday and promptly created a programme to calculate mortgage payments. Quick to recognise the gem before him, Koh's superior sent the young intern off to Hong Kong to write programs for a housing project for their client, Mobil.

All this happened before Koh even went to university.

When he eventually did further his education and complete his Masters at Harvard, Koh returned to Singapore and joined Hewlett Packard. Not surprisingly, he rose to the top post in the multinational company in Singapore.

"Three strikes and you're out"

One doesn't ride the storms of corporate crisis by being insulated from personal failures and fallouts. And Koh had his fair share of it early in his career as managing director of Hewlett Packard. His high-profile failures cost the company US$2 million, a princely sum in the 1980s. Mindful not to glorify failures, Koh asserted, "I don't wake up every morning feeling excited that I'm going to fail in something."

The first disappointment was a project that he initiated in hopes that he could make Singapore stand out to the head office in the US. It was a research project that had a lab manager in the US and the R&D team in Singapore. "It was almost management by remote control, travelling back and forth. The team wasn't sitting in the lab all day together with all of the people they were supposed to be working with. We were brand new at this game. We didn't understand the research process or the framework for it. With perfect hindsight, I would say it was doomed to failure," conceded Koh.

With lessons in the bag, a second project was launched. This time, the entire team was stationed in the US. But, as Murphy's law would have it, a competitor came up with an identical product — and sooner, six months earlier. His project was, subsequently, canned.

> I don't wake up every morning feeling excited that I'm going to fail in something.

"I remember a conversation with my boss' boss, who was head of International at that point in time, and he said, 'Three strikes and you're out,'" Koh recalled candidly on the drubbing he received.

Fortunately for him, the third strike was a home run. "So, I didn't have to quit," he said.

And it was from this background of failures and successes that he came to be handpicked to chair some of Singapore's largest government-linked organisations. First to come calling was SingTel where he held chairmanship in Asia's leading telecommunications company for 15 years, from 1986 to 2001. SIA came knocking and he chaired the board from 2001 to 2005, followed by one of Singapore's largest banks, DBS, from 2006 to 2010.

It was in SIA and DBS that he was thrown into the whirlpool of a regional epidemic that brought travel to a halt and a global financial shake up that was to drag the reputation of the bank through the mud.

Turbulence from the SARS epidemic

When Koh took on the role of chairman of SIA in 2001, the company was flying high as one of the most profitable airlines in the world, with profit growth of 30%. But in November 2002, in a village in Guangdong, China, one farmer's death started a chain of events that brought the aviation juggernaut to its knees, and indeed, many countries in Asia to a standstill.

SARS, or severe acute respiratory syndrome, typically starts as a form of pneumonia. In the outbreak of 2002, however, the spread of the disease from person to person was so widespread that it rapidly became a regional epidemic. The disease took almost 800 lives, mainly in Asia, with Singapore, Hong Kong, Vietnam, China, Taiwan, and the Philippines the worst hit.

A few months before the outbreak, another momentous event occurred that was to change the face of air travel to this day. On 11 September 2001, terrorists attacked the World Trade Centre in New York, flying two planes into the two landmarks. As significant a world event as that was, it was the SARS epidemic that affected SIA more adversely. 9/11, as the terrorist attack came to be known, affected all airlines around the world. But SARS targeted Asia alone through its spread.

> I can still remember planes being flown with one passenger!

"SARS was not a level playing field. It affected some airlines, those of us in Asia. It did not affect our competition in the rest of the world. Those are much more difficult problems to deal with because while you're spending your time sorting out your issues, others are moving on," he pointed out.

Travel advisories by the World Health Organization (WHO) were issued with Singapore, Hong Kong, China and Vietnam being placed on the list of infected areas. These notices caused widespread alarm as headlines reported new infections and deaths daily and brought travel to a standstill. During the crisis, in April and May, SIA lost about US$210 million, or about US$3.5 million a day. In fact, in April 2003, the load factor was a paltry 49% — planes were taking off half empty. "I can still remember planes being flown with one passenger! That was the record," Koh added.

To deal with the slowdown, several measures were introduced. Capacity was cut by 30% during the peak of the crisis, from March to June. For two months, 300 weekly flights were withdrawn, while capital expenditure and most non-critical projects were deferred or cancelled. On the labour front, for the first time in 20 years, SIA conducted a major retrenchment exercise. About 600 people lost their jobs. Pilots and cabin crew were forced to take unpaid leave. Staff who remained had their wages reduced by up to 16%, with management taking, in some cases, a 20% cut and board of directors, 50%.

As unpopular as the measures were, for Koh it was important to bolster the confidence of stakeholders amid the doom and gloom and keep the company's focus on the long haul. "I think in a crisis like that, what you need to do is to make sure that your people understand that the company is going to stand behind its business; that we are committed in the long run; that this, too, will pass. In other words, in a time of crisis, people need to know that the leaders themselves are confident."

To that end, the airline made a move that was counter-intuitive. The board voted at the height of the crisis to proceed with the US$100 million refurbishment programme to fit lie-flat seats, or *SpaceBeds*, on all its Airbus 777 planes. The programme was completed in June 2003 during the peak of the crisis. "That's a huge expression of confidence in the future of your own business," Koh said.

If there was a silver lining to the predicament, it was the speed at which the disease was contained the moment it was recognised as a global health threat. After its peak in April, the number of infections was drastically reduced and by July, the WHO lifted the advisories for the infected areas.

> In a time of crisis, people need to know that the leaders themselves are confident.

The few months of isolation among travellers saw pent-up demand the moment it was deemed safe to travel again. After the quarter of losses, SIA made up for some of the deficit in the next quarter with promotional fares and finally registering gains the third quarter onwards, ending the year with US$485 million in profit. Staff were repaid their salaries, lost through the wage cuts, and rewarded further with a 15% top up.

Steering DBS through a crisis of confidence

As global shifts and their subsequent aftershocks take place, economic cycles run their course and companies in one industry or another will take it in turns to make the headlines for crises of some sort.

For Koh, his next position after SIA saw him take on another debacle that no one could see coming, at least not in 150 years. And it all started in the US in 2003 when the housing bubble began, gradually leading to the mammoth bankruptcy of Lehman Brothers five years later.

While Wall Street was reeling from the spectacular losses as Lehman declared a US$619 billion debt, thousands of kilometres away, in Singapore, 10 financial institutions, including DBS, Merrill Lynch, Oversea-Chinese Banking Corporation (OCBC), and United Overseas Bank (UOB), were hit by the fiasco, too, having sold investment products issued by Lehman. At the bank's collapse, 10,000 retail investors who had invested US$350 million were affected.

To understand the selling point of Lehman's products, one need only look at the attractive returns of 5–6.5% paid out quarterly to those who invested in these structured deposits. This compared very favourably to fixed deposit rates that were sub 1%. The flip side, however, was that there were higher risks, with no guarantees that the principal would be secured. This, according to DBS, who had the most invested in Lehman, was clearly laid out to investors.

DBS had issued Lehman products to 4,700 customers in Singapore and Hong Kong amounting to US$250 million. Of these, 1,400 customers were from Singapore and were sold a product known as High Notes 5, all US$70 million of it. A month after Lehman sank, investors of the Notes were sent letters by DBS notifying them that their investments had come to naught.

The difference in the impact of the Lehman collapse on DBS and ICICI was in the parties who shouldered the losses. Even though ICICI had a substantial amount invested in Lehman through its London subsidiary, about US$80 million, the investment was in the form of senior bonds through its treasury operations. The losses were written off and, according to the bank, were "not material."[1] Sure, there was the few days of sheer panic with the bank run and the resultant squeeze on the bank's liquidity, but the bank was able to meet the demands of their customers for returns on their deposits and slowly rebuild its standing in the months ahead.

In the case of DBS, however, the losses were for their retail investors to bear, as stated in the terms and conditions of the investment, and with hundreds of victims clamouring for the return of their life's savings, the crisis took on a life of its own.

> What's legal and what's moral are not the same thing.

All hell broke loose as the bank's customers cried foul, claiming they were ill-advised. Retirees sobbed with stories of their life savings wiped out by relationship managers who, they alleged, did not explain the risks of the product. Others claimed they were misled by the bank. For the first time, investor activism was seen in the form of public protests as investors accused the financial institutions of misrepresentation. DBS was deemed irresponsible. How could investors, who could not even speak English well (an indication of a lower level of education in Singapore), be sold such complex products, critics asked. It was the classic David-and-Goliath duel — vulnerable small investor versus behemoth bank — that got the media, both online and mainstream, fired up in its coverage of the crisis.

One investor had claimed he didn't know his money was going to Lehman. "We thought all along that it was just like fixed deposits, very safe, but with a high interest rate. The bank representatives never told us that we could stand to lose so much, just like that."[2] The regulator was called in to adjudicate, which added further pressure on the financial institutions.

After acknowledging that it did not "meet the standards (it) upholds"[3] in some cases, DBS declared compensation of US$50 million to customers in Singapore and Hong Kong — some 20% of total losses.

Not content with the offer, 215 DBS investors filed a lawsuit to recover US$10 million. The suit declared that High Notes 5 was void when it was issued and as such the principal amounts were owing to the investors. The plaintiffs lost.

Seven years after the crisis, the chairman of DBS at the time had a philosophical response to the episode: "What's legal and what's moral are not the same thing," Koh mused.

He maintained that all the products associated with Lehman were "perfectly above board." However, it was a case of the fit of the products to the investors. "Was it exactly suitable for every single person that necessarily bought that? The answer is probably not," Koh conceded. "Is it correct that everybody who bought that was a victim of the bank? The answer is no. There were plenty of people who were perfectly aware of the risk, who took it; who, after the incident, all of a sudden became hardly educated in risks."

> I've never believed that hope is a good corporate strategy.

According to a statement from the bank, most of the customers who bought High Notes 5 weren't as vulnerable as they had been made out to be. The bank said two thirds of those who bought the product were its private banking customers, suggesting they were seasoned investors who had a minimum of US$140,000 in cash and/or investments with the bank. Furthermore, to debunk the perception that most of those burnt from the collapse were retirees, the bank said 80% were below 60 years of age.[4]

So, while the bank acknowledged its part in the losses, it made it clear that many customers were aware of the risks involved when they signed on.

To make matters worse, while the saga was unfolding, Singapore was experiencing its worst recession. GDP contracted by about 10% in 2009 from its peak. It was the first country in East Asia to fall victim to the Global Financial Crisis because of its trade-dependent economy.[5] It wasn't just the investors in Lehman-linked products that lost money, the country's two sovereign wealth funds, Temasek and GIC, also lost significant amounts. Temasek saw 30% of its portfolio value wiped out during the crisis. As a result of the downturn, DBS' profits dipped over two consecutive quarters.

Just as SIA went ahead with its *Spacebeds* in the middle of the SARS crisis, DBS, too, took proactive measures during the debacle to shore up investor confidence. "My natural instinct always is to act, rather than do nothing and hope. I've never believed that hope is a good corporate strategy," said Koh.

A rights issue was announced, offering existing shareholders one new share, at a 45% discount, for every two existing shares held. The exercise raised S$4 billion to boost the bank's balance sheet. The money raised went "to entrench our market position in key Asian markets and confidently weather the economic uncertainties ahead."[6] The move served to strengthen the bank and keep profits steady year on year despite the GDP contraction of 1.3%.

Dealing with the Black Swan

In 2007, writer and trader Nassim Nicholas Taleb released the bestseller, *The Black Swan*, on his theory of the occurrence of highly improbable events. Turning convention on its head, Taleb trades ostensibly on the basis of unexpected events taking place, or, as the analogy goes, black swans appearing. To this end, he would bet on those rare occasions when something extremely unusual happens — and make a windfall. Conversely, he would lose money on uneventful days.

Koh is wont to take a more pragmatic approach to the improbable, though not inconceivable: "If you live your whole life anticipating black swans, no organisation will move forward because no one will take a risk. And I don't think that is necessarily good for development. You have to accept that sometimes these things happen, you know. And that when it does happen, there are unpredictable things that result from it."

Reflecting on the DBS High Notes 5 debacle, Koh reckoned that the best strategy was responding to the circumstances with confidence-building measures rather than to wait it out. "Not to have acted and to have hoped, for example, that things would have bottomed out, that it can't get any worse, is not anticipating the tail risk of a black swan event."

***

I met Koh in his office in the R&D and technology hub of Singapore. The space his fund management company occupies is small relative to the large organisations he advised as chairman. It's a family-friendly office with children of staff buzzing around, idle from the school holidays. A handful of people were at their desks. A far cry from the clamour and commotion of yesteryear.

Koh has taken a backseat from his heyday but still travels widely. He has a little more time for leisure travel with his wife and friends while he indulges in photography. Some of his works adorn the walls of the office.

He brimmed with enthusiasm when he talked about some of the young entrepreneurs he advises and whose startups he invests in. He conceded he was better at recognising great ideas than creating them and his role today is to provide insights from his experience.

For all the bouquets and brickbats he's received in his high-profile past, Koh carefully chooses his words when asked what keeps him grounded today. "Both my two partners and myself, we are all Christians, so whatever is here, it's all temporary. Do we like to do well? The answer is yes. Will it be the be-all and end-all of our existence? The answer is probably no. We want our investors to make money, but are we willing to trample over everybody else to do it? The answer is no. We believe there's a proper way to conduct business. We want to conduct it as professionally as we can. We want to conduct it as morally as we can."

Words laden with much experience, born from a baptism of fire — a couple of times over.

Notes

1 "ICICI Bank has Rs 375 crore exposure in Lehman Brothers", Press Trust of India, 16 September 2008, <http://www.business-standard.com/article/finance/icici-bank-has-rs-375-crore-exposure-in-lehman-brothers-108091600053_1.html>

2 Koh Yi Na, "Angry investors turn up at Hong Lim Park to seek redress", The Online Citizen, 12 October 2008, <https://www.theonlinecitizen.com/2008/10/12/more-than-1000-people-at-speakers-corner/>

3 DBS Press Statement, 22 October 2008.

4 "DBS determined to uphold Standards; refined sales process in place", 8 July 2009, DBS News Release.

5 "Singapore is first East Asian country to slip into recession", History SG: an online resource guide, October 2008, <http://eresources.nlb.gov.sg/history/events/3cacf256-82cc-4776-b7f8-83757723b502>

6 DBS Press Statement, 22 December 2008.

Part VII

LEADER AS COMMUNICATOR

A mong Asia's business leaders, few stand out as well-rounded communicators — those who have the knack for reaching out to staff, partners, investors, government bodies, customers, media and public alike. Notably, the larger the audience, the greater the reticence. This is certainly not for the lack of opinions or insights. On a personal level, most have not honed the public speaking skills to capture the hearts and imaginations of their audiences. On a political level, it is safer to subject themselves to self-censorship for fear of unwittingly saying the wrong things.

Big business in Asia is an unwieldy creature. As growth progresses, so do regulations. Picking the right alliances in government and toeing the line of authoritarian regimes are keys to survival and growth.

At the same time, in today's environment of the 24/7 news cycle, the pervasive presence of social media and the unending commentaries of citizen journalists, the old adage that no news is good news doesn't hold. The norm has shifted to a free exchange of information and an expectation of openness and transparency among corporate leaders. Keeping lips sealed is *not* good news. Organisations whose leaders are accessible and integral to the company's corporate communication strategy are more favourably perceived than those who are seen as reactive and absent.

The guests I feature in this section have created their own personal brands through their success and charisma. They are seasoned spokespeople who have mastered the art of bridging their answers away from red-flagged topics. They are masterful storytellers, they possess an evident hubris and they take calculated risks to push the envelope. Their deftness in crafting strong messages, daring to be different and pushing for reforms, have benefitted them in measurable terms — through their bottom line, the removal of unfair industry practices and a high level of staff satisfaction. Of course, there have been instances when speaking up also came at a high cost.

Chapter 18

Now Everyone Knows Him

Tony Fernandes
AirAsia, Malaysia

Too big to fail. And too big to say no.

Nowhere is this more evident than in the case of AirAsia's Tony Fernandes, who launched one of Asia's most successful budget airlines with just two planes. He has always been held up as a charismatic leader, known for his outspoken and straight-talking rhetoric. But tracing his development from the time he started the business to my interview with him in 2014 to his latest and probably biggest miscalculation, after backing the wrong candidate in Malaysia's historic elections in May 2018, there is a progressive mellowing of the man.

It's an oft-told narrative that when one has little to lose, a certain devil-may-care persona gets to strut its stuff. But the moment the scales tip to a point where thousands of employees are dependent on the business and shareholders, from institutional to public, are holding you to account for their billions of dollars, the weight of responsibility causes leaders to weigh their words much more carefully.

If ever there was a businessman who has been loved and loathed for his words, one need look no further than Tony Fernandes.

***

When Fernandes first blazed onto the scene as a swaggering 37-year-old former music executive, with his flagship budget airline AirAsia, that declared magnanimously *Now Everyone Can Fly,* he ruffled a few feathers. He was there for media calls and promotions with his signature red AirAsia cap. He liberated the long-held duopoly between Singapore Airlines and Malaysia Airlines, plying the lucrative Singapore-Kuala Lumpur route, plunging the fares from US$400 for a return ticket to US$40, with taxes. Of course, while this was good news for the man in the street (and in the air), it also brought on the brickbats. Politicians and businesspeople with vested interests from both sides of the causeway derided him as a brash upstart whose venture was doomed to fail. After all, nothing like this had ever been done in Asia.

In 2001, Fernandes, with his partner Kamarudin Meranun, paid US$0.25 for two planes while taking on an US$11 million debt from DRB-Hicom, the company that started AirAsia without much success. With that came a throng of naysayers. Your quintessential underdogs.

Fernandes declared unabashedly that it was he who changed the face of aviation for the two countries. "If there wasn't a Tony Fernandes we would still be here with legacy airlines," he said, when I met him in 2014 at the former AirAsia Academy in Sepang, a stone's throw from the Kuala Lumpur International Airport (KLIA). "It would be Singapore Airlines and Malaysia Airlines. Since we started, there's Tiger, Jetstar, Lion. And I think we've created lots of jobs, lots of economy.

"So, I've upset a few people," he shrugged. "But if you balance it up, it's much better having low-cost carriers than just one type of airline, which it was before."

After 15 years, AirAsia has grown to a fleet of 200 planes flying over 250 routes with profits from year one, and this even during times when airlines were folding as rising jet fuel prices between 2011 and 2014 singed the competition of all, but the strong. In fiscal year 2016, the airline reported revenue of US$2.8 billion and net operating profit of US$385 million.

Today, AirAsia has expanded to bases in Thailand, the Philippines, Indonesia, India and Japan. Fernandes poses with his flight attendants, or his "Allstars," as he calls them, and hobnobs with world leaders,

> If there wasn't a
> Tony Fernandes we
> would still be here
> with legacy airlines.

including the Pope. He even won a public wager with his friend, Virgin's Richard Branson, who, as a result of losing the bet, served a day as a "stewardess" on an AirAsia flight, to the delight of the media. Not forgetting the many awards the industry has presented to Fernandes, including being recognised as Airline CEO of the Year for the third time by the global aviation organisation Centre for Aviation (CAPA) in 2016.

No filters

Fernandes' public relations team was very laid back when I had set up the interview with him. I suppose they could be since the boss is a PR maven himself. No one hovered over our conversation checking to see if anything needed to be censored. No boundaries were drawn before the interview. The boss was a big boy. He could handle himself. In fact, I put the invitation to be a guest on my show to him personally through email and he responded directly and promptly. Every TV producer's dream. But what deemed him a compelling profile for the show was his no-holds-barred, shoot-from-the-hip candour that made for great viewing and, for me as a host, an engaging conversation.

Fernandes was a colourful speaker with his unfiltered figures of speech. He was untainted by PR spiel and niceties. He said it as he saw it. Commenting on competitor Malindo, he opined that their "hybrid" model, seemingly straddling full-service and low-cost, was a dangerous position to be in: "You don't know whether they're gay or whether they're straight." And his view of how AirAsia came to be: "I always describe it with sexual terms. We were always a mistake in the government's eyes: they didn't abort us; they put us in a foster home. And I think we are very much now part of the family." Fernandes was also enamoured with Ratan Tata, the head of the Tata Group who is also his partner in AirAsia India. "I wasn't drawn to Tata Corporation as much as I was drawn to Ratan Tata. And when you walk around India, I feel very justified in my decision because people were kissing his toes, literally, in the Ministry of Finance. I've never seen anything like it." Then he quipped, "The closest I saw was Park Ji-sung in Korea, where they would kiss anything from him," referring to the former Manchester United footballer from South Korea.

Oh! And did I mention that he wasn't bashful? He declared himself "a brand ambassador for Malaysia." His loyalties, however, knew no national boundaries. If he believed in it, he would speak for it. As he did for a television commercial promoting Singapore, "which many people raised their eyebrows about," he deadpanned.

Because he had to

In all honesty, I had to work hard to keep my disinterest during the interview. Fernandes had a disconcerting habit of commending me for the questions I posed. At one point, he even said no one had asked him in all the years he'd been fronting the media a particular question I put to him on predicting trends. Call him a smooth operator, but here was a man who knew his way around journalists and was highly cognizant that we, too, had egos that could be stroked.

> I had to be forthright. If I wasn't, you wouldn't be sitting here talking to me.

This is all thanks to his exposure to the media from the beginning when he took over AirAsia and took on the incumbent operating environment that favoured two airlines above all others. "The only way I could get noticed was the press, to be honest, and speaking forthrightly, because you go and present and you get nowhere. The lobbies of the national carriers are phenomenal," he said. "So I had to be forthright. If I wasn't, you wouldn't be sitting here talking to me. We would have been long gone after right about a year."

It helps that Fernandes is articulate and his soundbites make for sensational quotes. His accent still holds traces of his British boarding school upbringing. Before heading off to Epsom College in England, he studied in an upper-class international school in Kuala Lumpur; the son of a doctor and a mother who sold Tupperware.

Not one to take things lying down, Fernandes had made bluntness his hallmark. He cried foul and protested publicly that "we are being stifled"[1] when in 2003, the Land Transport Authority of Singapore curbed his attempts to ferry AirAsia passengers by bus from Singapore to the budget carrier's southern hub in Johor's Senai Airport.[2] Fernandes also has a long-running feud with the main airport operator in Malaysia. He objected vociferously when the low-cost carrier terminal (LCCT) the airline had operated from for about a decade, was replaced by a new terminal, KLIA 2. He opposed the high airport tax at the new terminal and lamented the delays and cost overruns during construction.[3]

As much as he protested on every platform available to him, Fernandes has had to concede defeat in these clashes. Not only did he have to stop the bus services and fly direct to Singapore eventually, he's also not had his way with the airport operator, which is 50% owned by the government's investment arm, Khazanah. He had refused to move to KLIA2 beyond the deadline until the immigration and customs departments threatened to withdraw their services at the old terminal.

It's part of every entrepreneur's journey to win some and lose some. But it's the battles that they win that determine survival in the long haul. And it was Fernandes' battle royale with the Malaysian flag carrier that set the budget airline on its path to success.

Shortly after the launch of AirAsia, Malaysia Airlines saw its share of the domestic market shrink significantly. It was unfamiliar territory for the carrier that had dominated the Malaysian skies for over five decades, since 1947. They responded by slashing fares, sending a strong message that the price war was on. Fernandes saw red and inveighed against what he saw as unfair competition — there was no way AirAsia could survive the assault of an incumbent that was assisted by government subsidies, he insisted.

So desperate was he to level the playing field, Fernandes even gatecrashed an event to get the attention of the guest of honour, the Minister of Transport. He believed it was brazen stunts like these that got him the results he needed. After all the publicity he raised over the disparity, in 2006, the government, which was bearing losses of US$80 million a year for its national flag carrier,[4] declared the end of subsidies.

Looking back, Fernandes had no regrets going to town with his grievances. "I would have been bust, I can tell you that now. Malaysia Airlines would have destroyed us if I didn't go to the press and say this was unfair competition. There's no way you can compete with a state-subsidized airline. No way. We would have been long gone."

> If I was quiet, Malaysian Airlines would have crushed us.

"If I was quiet," Fernandes insisted, "Malaysian Airlines would have crushed us."

A social media maven

An AirAsia employee once jokingly mentioned that if you wanted to know what was happening to the company, follow the boss on Twitter. For any developments on AirAsia, reporters don't have to quote from a press release. Right off the bat is Fernandes himself on social media. He has over 1.5 million followers on Twitter who hear from him several times a day, over 600,000 on Facebook and 160,000 on Instagram.

His posts span a variety of themes — on the personal front he features his fitness programme, his daughter and friends. The same platforms are used to profile employees with special talents or achievements, news out of AirAsia and his English football team Queens Park Rangers and causes and issues he stands by. Occasionally, there're the outbursts with people and organisations that get his goat.

Fernandes' use of social media was at its exemplary best during the worst of times for AirAsia — the tragic crash of the flight 8501 in the Java Sea in December 2014, taking all 162 lives on board. It was Fernandes who appeared at the forefront of the crisis management team. He was prompt in providing updates as the tragedy unfolded and, at the same time, he was also the grieving face of the airline. The most poignant moments of the crisis came through Fernandes' tweets providing snapshots of his feelings:

> *Reality of seeing the evacuees and some of my aircraft parts are soul destroying;*
>
> *Been one of my toughest days. Spent a large part of day meeting families of passengers. Doing whatever we can;*
>
> *I'm arriving in Surabaya to take Nisa (crew member who perished) home to Palembang. I cannot describe how I feel. There are no words.*

As the man bared his soul to the world, there was no room for scepticism and criticism; only collective mourning.

AirAsia emerged from the crisis relatively unscathed, despite investigations pointing the finger at its plane and pilot. In fact, the crash did little to dent its reputation, judging from the award it picked up from

> I can't imagine some people in the world who don't mind being disliked and go out to be disliked.

Skytrax, often known as the Oscars of the aviation industry, the year after the incident. And it's been one award after another — 2017 was the ninth consecutive time the airline was recognised as World's Best Low-Cost Airline.

If there is a key to this hard-nosed businessman's personality that makes him the spokesman *par excellence,* as tempestuous as he may seem to be, it is, ironically, his predisposition towards people. People, he said, are what keep him going.

Fernandes enjoyed the attention he got from his staff at the airline's training centre where the interview was shot. He obliged us with a sequence of his interaction with his staff. Though the scene was orchestrated, the connections were genuine. He walked in on ongoing training sessions and joked with staff. Photos were snapped and faces were beaming.

Fernandes insisted it was important for him to be liked. "I read some of the press sometimes and people who don't know me say I'm arrogant. I'm completely the opposite!" he insisted. "I can't imagine some people in the world who don't mind being disliked and go out to be disliked."

The wrong bet

If being disliked was anathema to him, then it seemed out of character for Fernandes to stand against public opinion the way he did in the run-up to Malaysia's landmark general elections in May 2018. The polls brought down the only coalition the country had known since independence 61 years ago. Hostility against the incumbent government, led by the Barisan Nasional (BN), had been at its peak as citizens expressed frustration with the corruption of the government of Najib Razak and the rising cost of living. Added to that, the malapportionment of constituencies, the mid-week polling date and the disbandment of an opposition party at the last minute, further fanned the flames of ire among citizens.

After the polling date was announced, AirAsia made a pre-emptive move to shore up popular support by waiving all flight change fees for Malaysians travelling on May 9th, the day of the elections. Fernandes later offered more goodies — not only did he lower fares, he also added a further 120 flights across Malaysia that would carry 26,000 more passengers. All this to make sure Malaysians got to return to their home states to vote. The opposition party had stated that it needed at least 80% of registered voters to put in their ballot papers for it to see victory. While the people cheered, behind the scenes, several discussions led to a startling turn of events.

As campaigning by both coalitions got underway, Fernandes appeared early on in a photo opportunity with one of BN's candidates on his campaign trail. That incident passed quietly enough largely because Fernandes was accompanied by a bigger star in the eyes of Malaysians — world number one badminton player Lee Chong Wei. It was Lee that the media harped on and Fernandes received scant coverage. It was certainly nothing compared to what was to come.

As campaigning came to a head days before polling day, a video appeared of Fernandes attributing the success of AirAsia to the Najib government who had "put people first." That shocked many Malaysians. But it was the mammoth image that stood on the runway of Kuala Lumpur International Airport that stunned everyone. Malaysians were gobsmacked when pictures appeared on Najib's social media account of an AirAsia plane shrouded with the BN colours, splayed with its manifesto slogan across the livery of the Airbus 330 and stewardesses garbed in BN's blue instead of their signature red uniforms. To top it off, a photo emerged of Najib and Fernandes smiling for the camera on board the chartered flight from Kota Kinabalu to Kuala Lumpur.

Netizens did nothing to filter their disgust over what they saw as Fernandes' pandering to the authorities. The poster boy of Malaysian business success was pilloried for bootlicking. Speculation abounded. Many declared they were done with AirAsia.

In a video he released on his Facebook page days after BN's defeat, a tired and dejected Fernandes apologised for the "grave error of judgement," saying that he had "buckled in a crucial moment in our history." He revealed that he was backed into a corner. He was told by the Prime Minister's Office to remove the Chairman of AirAsia X, Rafidah Aziz, a vocal critic of BN and a strong supporter of the opposition. He refused. Fernandes also claimed that the Malaysian Aviation Commission (MAVCOM) had instructed him to cancel the extra flights that were to ferry Malaysians back to vote. He refused. He only did what he had to to appease the government, he said.

Since then, many have had a change of heart as sympathisers like Rafidah herself came alongside in a show of a support for an injured comrade. Opinion was divided as many wondered if Fernandes would have apologised if BN had remained in power. Others continued to insist that he was a political opportunist playing victim.

After the apology video was released, MAVCOM lodged a police report against Fernandes saying his accusations were "baseless and malicious." The regulator insisted that it did not instruct any airline to cancel or reduce flights during the elections. AirAsia quickly responded by saying they had evidence to prove otherwise.

Being a man who enjoys popularity, the video was Fernandes' attempt at buying back some of the love that he had lost from the *rakyat,* or citizens. But in trying to control the damage, he added fuel to the fire. Not only did it reignite the anger among Malaysians over what they saw as his sycophantic ways, the spat between AirAsia and MAVCOM continued to play out, keeping Fernandes in the news for all the wrong reasons.

Corporate communication strategists can debate over the necessity of the apology. He could've let the mistake of speaking up for BN die a natural death. After all, days before the apology, a politician from the new government had revealed the reason for Fernandes' stunt, making him out to be a hero, a lamb led to the slaughter.

Wittingly, or not, Fernandes threw his hat into the political rink with his offer of more flights and lower fares. Unfortunately for him, that put him on two sides of the political divide — a dangerous place to be. It was political naiveté that led him to believe that he was being neutral in speaking up for Najib in the video. While it was a costly miscalculation on his part, the episode is a reminder that large organisations have little to gamble with.

Gone are the days when Fernandes can give a tongue lashing to the authorities the way he did when AirAsia was in its infancy. The straight-talking maverick has been trapped by his own success. By his own admission, he had much less influence in the previous elections because he just wasn't as big a name as he is today. Ironically, the airline's growth has muzzled its formerly pugnacious founder, moulding him into a shadow of his past self.

Until there are distinct lines that protect businesses from government in politics, businessmen in big leagues like Fernandes, will have to be more cautious about airing their opinions. Being communicative is one thing, walking the talk becomes a hodgepodge of stepping stones on quicksand.

In this crisis of confidence, Fernandes can call on the social capital he has built up over the years as a star communicator and the pride of Malaysians. He can continue to reach out to his millions of social media followers. He will find his unique and winsome ways to bare his soul to disarm the fiercest critic. And for as long as AirAsia continues to fly the national flag high and provide an indispensable service to most Malaysians, it won't be long before they would forgive, even if they won't forget, this episode.

But for this straight-talking tycoon, speaking out will certainly be a much more calculated move, as he weighs the various quarters of the court of public opinion. And the stakes will only get higher, the higher he flies.

Notes

1 Goh Chin Lian, "AirAsia boss raps S'pore over bus links to Senai", The Straits Times, 24 October 2003.

2 Fernandes had put off plans to fly to Singapore's Changi International Airport, citing the high cost there as an impediment to his low-cost model. Senai is about 30 kilometres from the border and with the bus services, passengers could hop on to the ride from the central business district and get to Senai in an hour — with loads of savings in air fare to boot. The Singapore government stood firm against the bus services leading AirAsia eventually to fly direct to Singapore in 2008 from Kuala Lumpur.

3 Fernandes hasn't let up on his frustrations with the airport authorities — he's complained about the new runway, which he deemed unsafe (he tweeted: "*sad that my ceo @aireenomar has to waste her time keep going to malaysia airports to sort something that should never have happened*") and most recently, he lambasted the operator for its lack of facilities (on Facebook, he posted "*Honestly, I am really fed up with Malaysia Airports. They promised us bag drop in July. 30 machines. Zero, and now they say no budget!*")

4 Vijay Joshi, "Malaysia Airlines Loses Subsidies, Routes", Associated Press, 27 March 2006.

Chapter 19

The Cross-dresser Chairman

Allan Zeman

Lan Kwai Fong Group & Ocean Park, Hong Kong

W hen Allan Zeman arrived in Hong Kong from Canada in 1975, it wasn't to seek his fortune. He already had that from importing clothes from the then British colony to Canada. But it was the opportunity to "service the world market" in Hong Kong that lured the ambitious young entrepreneur at 26, to leave his home for this faraway land of opportunity.

Instead of building a trading business, however, it was something else that drew his attention. Where most people could only see the district of Lan Kwai Fong then as a run-down, dingy backwater better known as a hub for flower shops and marriage arrangers, Zeman saw opportunity. He began buying property in the area, slowly but surely, at a bargain, since the location was considered the outskirts. Before long, he bought up enough property to develop the locale into a niche party hub that drew locals and expats looking for a fun night out.

Today, Lan Kwai Fong has become a must-visit entertainment destination with 100 bars and restaurants. The properties occupy premium space in land-scarce Hong Kong.

By the 1990s Zeman had established himself as a well-respected property magnate who had proven his mettle. As the man with the party wand, he was sought after not just by business partners but by the Hong Kong government as well. After all, if he could transform a dilapidated district into a world-renowned entertainment centre, he could weave his magic, too, on a jaded national icon to bring it back to its former glory days. Couldn't he?

An icon turned eye-sore

> They are all after me for Lan Kwai Fong.

Zeman was late for our interview. He was at the doctor's clinic nursing a sore throat. He turned up dressed in his trademark crisp white shirt with upturned collar, but sounding and looking a little worse for wear. Yet, he forced a smile, welcomed us and with a little warming up, the affable businessman found his mojo and was in top form regaling me with his stories.

And as with all storytellers who've earned their stripes, Zeman is wont to indulge in a little self-promotion as he talked about the Chinese government "chasing me from as far north as Harbin, Shenyang, Wuhan, you name the city. They are all after me for Lan Kwai Fong" and as he related an incident about sitting in a café in Chengdu and being recognised, "as everyone does in China."

These are not empty boasts, however, as the Lan Kwai Fong Group has, over the last three decades, grown into a niche and formidable property player known for its entertainment and lifestyle brand. And truth be told, to sit at the pinnacle of an industry, entrepreneurs invariably embody a certain chutzpah that comes with being audacious enough to dream and live big.

Zeman's knack for bringing a buzz to his developments, drawing party-goers like moths to a flame, has attracted partners who want that same magic in their properties. Enter Chengdu, Shanghai, Wuxi, Hainan, and Phuket where the Group has expanded. Its latest project in Shanghai is DreamCentre, a US$2.4 billion entertainment, retail, and cultural playground that will open in 2018.

And it was Zeman's ability to turn water into wine that made him the go-to man to breathe new life into a fading theme park that the Hong Kong government was desperate to save.

Ocean Park opened its doors in 1977 to great fanfare. It was a novel combination of an amusement and marine park. It relied on this positioning for many years until a new generation of well-travelled Hongkongers began to tire of the place as it became jaded and rundown. Visitor numbers dwindled and its future became bleaker with each foundation stone set by the soon-to-be-open Hong Kong Disneyland.

Ocean Park was of national significance and the government could not allow it to shut down. Something had to be done. And someone special had to do it. The chief executive of Hong Kong at that time knew just who that would be.

"When Tung Chee-hwa called me, he said, 'I need your help,'" recalled Zeman of the call he received from the top government official. "'I need you to go to look at Ocean Park. We don't know what to do with it.'"

Zeman's response was far from enthusiastic: "I said to him 'You are crazy! I've never been there.' But he was very persistent. He called me six times. By the sixth time, I was telling him I better give him face. It's the chief executive calling."

Zeman's first tentative steps to Ocean Park confirmed his suspicions. "What I saw was an old park. It was falling apart. The paint was peeling. The pavement was falling apart. Nobody was spending money upgrading the park."

He could've walked away from this onerous task but it was the significance of Ocean Park that was too big to ignore. "It would be a crime to close the park because so many people grew up with Ocean Park. It had a generational value," Zeman said, conscious that Hongkongers who went there as children were returning there with *their* children.

After some thought, he got back to Tung. "I said, 'If I don't take the job, who will you give it to?' He said, 'I don't really have anybody except a government official.' 'Well,' I said, 'you may as well close the park then as Disney is coming.'" So, with the weight of the country's heritage on his shoulders and the assurance of support from Tung, Zeman took on the job.

The more he delved into the park, the more he found unique aspects that he could build on. Once again, where others saw obstacles, Zeman discovered opportunities. "I loved that it was on the hillside. And the previous CEO was complaining that it was difficult to operate *because*

> I loved that it was on the hillside and the previous CEO was complaining that it was difficult to operate because it was on a hillside!

it was on a hillside!" he remarked. Zeman went on to enthuse, "It had a cable car! It was overlooking Deep Water Bay! And when I got off the cable car and I saw the billion-dollar view, I thought 'My God! That's so amazing.'"

As Zeman's excitement about Ocean Park's potential grew, so did his vision for it. He took on the role of chairman with such vigour that embodying the new identity of the park became more than just a figure of speech.

Taking the mickey out of himself

One of Zeman's first tasks at Ocean Park was to overhaul the management team. He brought in a CEO with relevant experience. Not one to do things by halves, he then set a new direction. "Even though it was a government-run park at that time, I thought to myself, we have to be world class." A US$710 million masterplan was put in place to revive the park, doubling the number of attractions from 35 to over 70.[1]

Zeman also set about distinguishing Ocean Park from Hong Kong Disneyland as an animal theme park — with surprises every day. "I thought to myself, if I go to a Disney attraction one day — and they do it very well — it's mechanical. And if I go back the next day, it is going to be the same attraction. In Ocean Park, if I go and see the pandas one day, they are fighting, and the next day, they are hugging. And if I go back the next day they are hanging from a tree. So, I always say, 'Expect the unexpected!'"

To tug at the heartstrings of Hongkongers and instil a sense of belonging and pride in the new Ocean Park, Zeman coined the unofficial moniker, the People's Park.

When it finally came time to relaunch the attraction, the team was at its wits end. How do you go to town with the new-look Ocean Park without the pomp and pageantry that would come with a hefty price tag?

"We did not have the money that Disney had and we were just trying to survive. We needed to give the media something interesting that we are selling," said Zeman, of being backed into a corner.

What if I dressed like a jellyfish?

Forced to be radical in his approach, Zeman announced to the marketing team that he would do something that had never been done by anyone in Hong Kong, much less the chairman of the organisation! Tough times with small budgets called for outrageous measures.

"Ocean Park as a theme park is about fun and fantasy. I thought to myself very quickly, 'What if I dressed like a jellyfish?'" Zeman recalled. "(The marketing team) asked, 'Are you kidding?' I said, 'No.' And I didn't think twice." At least, that's what he thought until the day of the media launch.

"On the day of the press conference, all the press was outside with the photographers and I came to the park and I saw the four little girls dressed up in their costumes in the dressing room and they had my jellyfish costume. I tried it on, looked in the mirror and I looked ridiculous and thought, 'There is no way in the world that I can go out looking like this!'"

"But then in Rome, you do as the Romans do. And I went out there and the press turned wild and they were taking pictures. The next day on the front page in every newspaper, not only in Hong Kong but all around the world — Seattle, Washington, Sydney, Bangkok — *The chairman of Ocean Park dressed as a jellyfish!* I realised at that time that this is really great advertising!"

Consistency in branding right down to appearances was key, explained the irrepressible businessman. "If I am the chairman of a bank," he said, "Of course, I would be wearing a suit and tie, be very prim and proper. But Ocean Park, as a theme park, is about fun and fantasy!"

Zeman didn't stop with that opening act. He had since dressed as a Caribbean dancer (with heels!), a panda, Shoulao — the god of longevity, a ghost bride, and the list goes on. And the public got the message: Ocean Park was all about fun, surprise, and just letting your hair down. The revived theme park drew the crowds back as people became curious about the new face of an old icon. And they liked what they saw. Where visitor numbers were hovering at the three-million mark pre-Zeman, the number had more than doubled while he was chairman, surpassing seven million. Translated, from a deficit of US$500,000 in 2003, the park turned in a surplus of US$16 million in 2013.[2]

About six months after I met with Zeman, reports surfaced of attempts to remove him as chairman of Ocean Park, a position he had held for 11 years. Rumour had it that it was a political decision because he had supported Henry Tang for the chief executive post in the 2012 elections in Hong Kong. Tang's rival Leung Chun-ying eventually won. Zeman, however, chose to believe that it was a regulation that limited terms of office bearers in statutory boards. Whatever it was, he was in the dark about why he was removed in June 2014.[3]

Zeman was clearly unhappy with the decision. After all, he had turned the waning park into a bustling wonderland. Zeman was so instrumental in driving the renewed success of the theme park that he became known as "the Mouse Killer," referring to how he gave Hong Kong Disneyland (and its mascot) a run for its money. The plan to save Ocean Park was one of those stories that Zeman never tires of telling.

Putting his face to his brands

It was Halloween when my crew and I visited the Park and the place was bustling with partygoers and families taking a mid-week night out to join in the festivities. Life had certainly returned to Ocean Park.

Interestingly, not too far away, in Lan Kwai Fong, another party was happening on a much louder and creepier scale. This party hub has become synonymous with Halloween and New Year's Eve festivities. And Hongkongers and expatriates have Zeman to thank for this hobnobbing space.

When Zeman first introduced Halloween to Hong Kong, the locals looked askance at the expatriates who donned strange costumes on that night of the year. But with time and with the hallmark Zeman style of continually pushing the envelope, Halloween has become a major event in the tourist calendar in Hong Kong.

As a master creator, Zeman is constantly thinking one step ahead. To him, it's all about setting higher goals. Set yourself up for first class, he said, and the least you'll get is business. But if your aim is only business class, then economy is what you're saddled with.

This relentless push for the best has led Zeman to *become* the brand he has built. Think Lan Kwai Fong and images of a grinning, shaven *gwailou* smiles back at you — in his signature white shirt with upturned collar. His image is also used in the company's mobile play app, complete with stickers plastered all over it.

Allan Zeman isn't your typical Asian entrepreneur (perhaps, being Canadian by origin accounts for that). His willingness to engage with the public has struck the right notes. He holds no punches when taking the mickey out of himself and he is an engaging storyteller. Couple that with his hard-nosed business sense and his unrelenting vision for the best, and you have enterprises that never fail to delight his customers — and by default — his investors, too.

However, Zeman does draw a line at embodying his brands entirely. He's a teetotaller. And in the world of entertainment that he sits atop, this, ironically, sets him up as an oddity.

"The father of Lan Kwai Fong, believe it or not, doesn't drink," he revealed, referring to himself by the unofficial title he's been given. "He only drinks water. He doesn't drink any alcohol."

Not that this should surprise anyone. When it comes to Allan Zeman, you'll just have to expect the unexpected.

Notes

1   "Ocean Park Unveils Its Redevelopment Strategy to Maximise Edutainment Experience Hong Kong's Financial Secretary joins the Park family to celebrate Ocean Park's Master Redevelopment Plan symbolic groundbreaking ceremony", Ocean Park Press Release, 23 November 2006.

2   Phila Siu, "Allan Zeman says he's being forced out of top job at Ocean Park", South China Morning Post, 23 June 2014, <http://www.scmp.com/news/hong-kong/article/1538995/allan-zeman-reveals-anger-being-forced-out-ocean-park-chairman?page=all>

3   "Zeman says he's being forced out of top job at Ocean Park", South China Morning Post, 23 June 2014.

Chapter 20

The Sunday Email Leader

Liew Mun Leong
CapitaLand & Changi Airport Group, Singapore

In 2012, the Institute of Public Relations of Singapore named the CEO of CapitaLand "Outstanding PR Champion of the Year." On receiving the notice, the head honcho, Liew Mun Leong, sheepishly admitted he hadn't heard of the organisation, much less, the award. But he decided to accept it in order not to appear arrogant nor exhibit poor PR skills.[1]

Among the leaders of the biggest companies in Singapore, one man holds his own, both as the executive who built one of the largest property players in Asia and as the voice of conscience for the industry, the latter being a rare attribute among the technocrats who fill the executive suites.

At 68, when I met him in 2014 at the Chairman's office in Changi Airport, Liew Mun Leong's speech was peppered with pragmatism that comes from being linked with the Singapore government for the last four decades. Yet, he also exuded an affability of a man who genuinely enjoys good company (yes, present company included), even if that came with a camera crew and the requisite set.

Liew has been chairman of the much-lauded airport since 2009, but it was his role as the founding president and CEO of CapitaLand that brought him to the public eye. He held the position at CapitaLand for 12 years until his retirement in 2013.

A man who holds his own

I had heard much about Liew from interviews he'd given; through the letters he had written faithfully every week to his 12,000 employees at CapitaLand, which were selectively compiled into four volumes of a book; as well as through personal exchanges with people who've worked with him.

What was it about the man that would make him instrumental in building CapitaLand to one the biggest real estate players in Asia with over US$50 billion in real estate assets in 2012 (and along the way reap the benefits of being the highest paid CEO in Singapore at the time), envision China in the 1980s as the catalyst for growth for the company, include some of the most influential political and business leaders in Singapore in his inner circle, and stand out as one of the more outspoken local CEOs?

After all, here is a man who defies the typical profile of leaders in Singapore Inc. He speaks English with a colloquial accent, sprinkles his speech with Chinese proverbs, and has no elite school backing to his name. But none of that obviously matters when he has sharp entrepreneurial instincts, strong leadership acumen, and an ease in connecting with people.

Speaking his mind

Liew started work as an engineer in the 1970s when he worked on Singapore's first airport in Paya Lebar, before he helped build the runway of the present one in Changi. He climbed the ranks over time and headed the Singapore Institute of Standards and Industrial Research, a statutory board to promote industrial R&D. Later the opportunity to run a government-linked real estate company, Pidemco, came knocking. In 2000, Pidemco merged with DBS Land to form CapitaLand and Liew became the new entity's founding CEO.

Liew is part of the inner circle of the founding father of Singapore, the late Lee Kuan Yew, having regular dinners with him right up to the weeks before Mr Lee was taken to the hospital for the last time. In fact, Liew was one of the few invited to keep vigil by Mr Lee's casket during the wake at Sri Temasek and to the private family funeral service. Liew's affection and respect for the late Mr Lee extends to a large painted portrait of the first Prime Minister in his office. Ever the connector, he even pulled together the best in his contact list — including Asia's top businessmen, Robert Kuok and Li Ka-shing, and former chief justice of Singapore, Yong Pung How — to have them write their own personal story of Mr Lee in a collection of memoirs published in 2016.

Liew is popular with the local media, not just for the weight he carries when he speaks, but also the ease in which he speaks out — unwavering opinions that, as all opinions go, make a stand for some and take a position against others. This, in the placid corporate communication environment like Singapore's, makes for good news stories.

During the height of the Global Financial Crisis in 2008, DBS, Singapore's biggest bank, retrenched some 900 employees. DBS is part owned by the CapitaLand's parent company, sovereign wealth fund Temasek. In an interview shortly after the announcement, Liew said laying off staff was "morally wrong" and it was costs, not staff, that should be cut.[2]

Behind the scenes, there must have been some rumblings as a week after Liew's interview was published, he had to clarify that he had been referring to lay-offs in the *real estate industry* where staff costs were relatively low and lay-offs were, therefore, unwarranted. Regardless of the context of his comments, Liew won plaudits for speaking against the unpopular move.

In another instance that divided popular opinion, Liew spoke out against the trend of shoebox units, or apartments less than 500 square feet. True to the maxim that if you build it, people will buy it, especially in land-scarce Singapore, small investors began pumping their savings into these properties. As supply increased, A buzz was created around these affordable units in the small island state with one of the world's costliest real estates. The lower quantum paid for these units, however, masked the higher-than-usual price per square foot. Purchases for these tiny apartments reached an all-time high in 2012, at US$2700 per square foot.[3]

The government by then had started to sound a note of caution. Liew, however, was not as tentative in his comments. He insisted that families should not be reduced to living in such small spaces, calling it

> You move on to the next runway. So, I've learnt to be very dispassionate about such things.

"almost inhuman" and that he was "dead against" these units.[4] Seen against his background, growing up in a one-room rental shared by seven family members, Liew's remarks seemed almost personal.

Indeed, statement went on to cause not a little stir in a country where leaders of large local corporations are normally tight-lipped and reticent in their communication with the public, especially when it pertained to the activities of their competitors.

Four months later, the Singapore government put a curb on these developments declaring them a strain on local transport infrastructure.

Not everyone, however, shared his opinion. After Liew stepped down, CapitaLand reversed his decision and began building these units again. When I suggested that the developments had been selling well, judging from the number of units coming on stream and that he could've been wrong, Liew wouldn't budge. "I'm not really sure they've done very well with that in the first instance." He went on to maintain, "I've got enough psychologist reports, five to six reports, that say it's not healthy for the family to live in a shoebox. So, I'm not sure long term they've done well."

Was Liew disappointed with the U-turn on his decision? "After 2012, it's a chapter closed for me. You move on to the next runway. So, I've learnt to be very dispassionate about such things," he said, stonewalling my attempts to get closer to a raw nerve.

It's all about people

At the time of our interview, Liew had left CapitaLand for one and a half years but remained busy in his roles as chairman of Changi Airport and government-linked urban planner Surbana Jurong. He lectures occasionally at the National University of Singapore as provost chair professor in the business school and the engineering faculty. Not forgetting, overseeing his personal investments in several eateries, including the Michelin chain of Tim Ho Wan restaurants in Singapore. Retirement is not in his vocabulary.

"My concept of retirement is when you drop dead," he deadpanned.

Liew connects easily with people. Those who've worked with him speak well of him. His ability to engage with people goes hand in glove with his firm belief in their development.

Liew has taken on the idea of "planting fruits in other people's trees," a concept he came across in *Finishing Well,* a book by Bob Buford, on living the second half of life. His contribution to students is his way of planting fruits. "This is actually very enjoyable when you see bright-eyes bushy-tails talking to you and they say, 'I want to be this. I want to be that.' It's very satisfying to tell them 'Look don't be impatient. You have 44 years to work before you reach my time.' Sharing some of the experiences, I think, is very gratifying."

My concept of retirement is when you drop dead.

Training and development is nothing new to Liew. Since 1990, he has taken it upon himself to mentor a group of about eight potential leaders for three years at a time. This was a practice he learnt from the late Lee Kuan Yew, who was known to identify top political figures at the early stages of their careers and making them his political secretaries.

As CEO of CapitaLand, Liew also spearheaded the setting up of a training school, CapitaLand Institute of Management and Business (CLIMB). CLIMB was established in Shanghai as well, to see to the training needs of staff in China. Taking it a step further, Liew even made it a point to be a trainer at the Institute's Management and Leadership course for mid- and senior-level staff.

Additionally, he would make time for quarterly town hall meetings with staff, including Q&As from those present and those watching through webcast. When he visited offices overseas, communication sessions with local staff would be a part of his itinerary.

In one of his emails to staff in 2011, Liew wrote:

"We have to learn to speak our minds to do our jobs well. If you do not, the company cannot understand you and know how you can contribute. Everyone must speak up, whatever their position in the company may be. Managers and leaders will need to be even more communicative because if you are not, your staff will never understand what you have in mind. You cannot manage or lead effectively if you do not speak up."[5]

The emails have been compiled into four volumes of a book, *Building People: Sunday Emails from a CEO.* These missives contain

> **There's no such thing as an uncommunicative leader.**

Liew's insights on management, politics, and life, mostly through his interactions with people and his personal journey. He used these emails to give notice to staff on his expectations and the culture that he wanted to build in the company.

"It started off in '98 when one Sunday I wrote about something and I sent it through email," he said. "And I discovered that whatever I wrote in the email can, with a press of a button, be promenaded to 10,000–12,000 people all over the world. And I find that this is a very effective way of getting my staff to understand what I'm thinking."

"I seriously think that the corporate culture of an organization is very much driven by the leaders. And for the leader to make himself known as to what he thinks are the core values or culture of the company, he needs to express himself. There's no such thing as an uncommunicative leader."

In one of his letters, Liew pointed out that business leaders in our part of the world were guilty of "under-communicating" and called on them to "be brave about facing the media," to be "friendly with journalists," and "enjoy a good interview," all of which he practices well.

I once goaded, half in jest, a senior director at a CapitaLand subsidiary into conceding that he didn't really take these letters seriously, that they were just the musings of a boss whom he could not but pander to. But he didn't take the bait. Instead, the executive genuinely reported that they *were* useful and enjoyable.

***

A common characteristic of leaders who are great communicators is their mutual interest in people. They are energised when they interact with others, they have a loyal following and they possess a certain vulnerability that makes them winsome. At the same time, they speak with a bluntness that can offend some people. Then again, who ever said leadership is a popularity contest?

Even after withdrawing from his executive role, Liew has continued his weekly staff memos, this time to staff of Changi Airport and Surbana Jurong. And as "active non-executive chairman" of Changi

Airport, a title he jokes Temasek has informally given him, he carries on his personal interest in developing "human capital" while overseeing development and policies.

You can't put a good man down, as they say.

Notes

1 Liew Mun Leong, *Building People: Sunday Emails from a CEO*, Vol 3 (John Wiley & Sons, 2013), 43.

2 "When times are bad, prepare for good times", Straits Times, 3 December 2008.

3 "Shoebox Units — Everybody's Watching 'Em", Squarefoot Research, <https://www.squarefoot.com.sg/market-watch/shoebox-units>

4 Pooja Thakur and Haslinda Amin, "CapitaLand CEO Calls Shoebox Apartments Inhuman", Bloomberg, 24 May 2012.

5 Leong, *Building People*, 122.

Part VIII

PHILANTHROPY

While charitable works are commonplace in Asian societies, philanthropy, as a structured and institutionalised practice only began to see the light of day in the last decade. This is due to the exponential growth in the number of billionaires in this part of the world. Also, thanks to organisations that have mushroomed to help givers direct their money to activities that maximise impact, more of the well-heeled are beginning to consider paying it forward with their wealth. Private banks such as UBS, Credit Suisse, and Coutts have also, in the last few years, set up their philanthropy advisory divisions in the region to help their ultra-high-net-worth (UHNW) clients who, in a manner of speaking, don't quite know what to do with their money.

In a 2015 report by Coutts, one of the UK's oldest private banks, the three biggest givers in Asia on its list — China, Hong Kong, and Singapore — recorded a combined total of US$6.8 billion. What's significant is that while the number of givers of over US$1 million is relatively small in Asia, at over 350, compared to over 1000 in the US, the average amount given is high, ranging from US$21 million to US$26 million. The average big donor in the US gave about half of that, or US$13 million.[1] At the same time, the amount of donations among the big Asian givers increased by close to 60% over a year. So, the indicators are positive for the growth of philanthropy in the region.

Among the causes that receive the most donations are higher education and healthcare. Interestingly, more funds are being directed to foundations as more are set up, suggesting that donors are taking a more systematic approach to giving. Credit Suisse Private Banking Asia Pacific reported a 10-fold increase in the number of foundations they helped establish, up to 30, over a period of five years.[2]

Invariably, guests on my show are always keen to talk about their charitable causes. As a journalist, my role is to balance their enthusiasm with the real impact of their work. Then there's also the scepticism of charity positioned as a public relations exercise. So, when approaching the angle of philanthropy, I'm always armed with a healthy dose of curiosity more than endorsement.

In this section, I highlight two givers who have made headlines by the sheer size of their donations. One, to a single cause that he's sold out on and giving through a structure that he hopes will continue to be a source of funding for posterity. The other, driven by his faith, gives to various causes, spurred on by a simple philosophy on giving.

Chapter 21

A Foundation for the Mind

Jeffrey Cheah
The Jeffrey Cheah Foundation and Sunway Group, Malaysia

Between academics and businessmen, Malaysian billionaire Jeffrey Cheah prefers the company of the former. He is inspired by their conversations and is thrilled when he hears complex concepts explained simply. It helps, too, he says, that they want nothing from him.

So, one of the personal benefits of having an education foundation is the opportunity Cheah gets to listen and learn from academics of the highest repute from Harvard, Cambridge, and Oxford, which happen to be universities he collaborates with. And you get the feeling that Cheah takes pride in being associated with academia when three quarters of his biography on the Sunway Group's website lists his involvement in education. This despite having 12 business divisions with a combined market capitalisation of US$4 billion under his watch.

Cheah had a complexion that belied his 69 years when I met him in 2014. He moved with his posse of people about him. He made sure he sussed me out before the interview with lunch beforehand. The topic of conversation, as was ever the talking point in Malaysia — politics. Sarena, Cheah's daughter and likely successor joined us at the table; she was pleasant but deferential. Here was a man who knew his place, as did others around him.

But could I expect anything less from one of Malaysia's most successful entrepreneurs?

The founder of the Sunway Group, a conglomerate with interests in property development, construction, healthcare, retail, leisure, and education, is one of Malaysia's richest men worth about US$900 million. The gold mine that set him off on the path to riches was really a disused tin mine, all 800 acres of land pock-marked with mining pools before its transformation.

From wasteland to wonderland

Cheah grew up in the small town of Pusing in the state of Perak, about 200 kilometres from the capital. The Kinta Valley, where he lived with his large family, was the largest producer of tin ore in the first half of the 20th century. Cheah's father held the sublease to a tin mine in the 1960s. He did well enough to send his son to Victoria University in Australia.

When Cheah returned to Malaysia after his business studies, he worked with his father for six months. But differences of opinions led him away from the family business. He landed a job as an accountant for a motor assembly plant in Kuala Lumpur. That lasted a few years until he began to feel restless.

"I can't report to people," he admitted. "I wanted to be on my own."

So, in the 1970s, he went back to what he knew best — tin mining. With some help from his father, he bought 500 acres of tin mines about 20 kilometres from Kuala Lumpur. The cost of the land — about US$120,000, paid up over three years.

Seeing a further opportunity in the development of the capital city and its vicinity at the time, Cheah quarried the rocks dredged up during the mining process and produced stone and sand for construction. That side business turned out to be a veritable cash cow.

At the back of his mind, however, Cheah had a strong suspicion that his mainstay, the tin mines, would reach the end of its lifespan soon. He began to look at other ways to work the land. In 1980, he applied to convert the land from mining to property development, paying the government US$0.40 per square foot for the lease. Sunway City, one of Malaysia's most successful townships, began taking shape.

As Cheah anticipated, by the mid-1980s the price of tin tanked and the death knell tolled for the industry in Malaysia.

With permit in hand to transform the business, Cheah's vision, however, was a hard sell. While he saw a thriving integrated development where people lived, worked, and played, bankers saw the deep holes of the mining pools and balked at the cost of filling them. The loose earth inherent in the tin mining land was also difficult to build on.

> It's nice after visions are realized but the journey was a long, long one. I had lots of sleepless nights.

Looking back, Cheah mused, "It's nice after visions are realized but the journey was a long, long one. I had lots of sleepless nights."

The investment was deemed such a liability, Cheah had difficulty securing loans to start the development. There were the few who did back him up and their decisions paid off handsomely. Property valuations in Sunway today range from US$200 per square foot for a new condominium to US$500 per square foot for a commercial property.

Cheah is fond of recalling a visit by Singapore's founding Prime Minister Lee Kuan Yew to Sunway in 2004. He often reiterates the honour that Lee accorded him when he praised Cheah for turning his model township from "a wasteland into a wonderland."

Since the early days, Sunway has been transformed into a town built, owned and operated by the Group with residential and commercial properties, a theme park, mall, hospitals and schools. Beyond Malaysia, the Group has extended its reach to China, Singapore, and other Southeast Asian countries. Consolidated revenue was over US$1 billion in 2016.

Recently, the opportunity to repeat its success in Sunway City came knocking; this time in the southern part of the peninsula, in Johore. In a joint venture with the country's sovereign wealth fund, Khazanah Nasional, Sunway Property is developing 1,800 acres of land in the new enclave of Iskandar with a gross development value of US$7.8 billion.

A legacy in perpetuity

Every organisation has its sacred cow — the one project that holds a special place in the boss' heart. The education division of the Sunway

Group is that golden child. Not only is it the only one of the 12 business divisions that remains unlisted, it is also one of the initial businesses set up after the first homes were built in Cheah's flagship project. It was years later that the leisure, hotel, retail, and healthcare divisions were formed.

In 1987, Sunway College began providing opportunities for Malaysians to pursue overseas tertiary education through its twinning programmes. This allowed students to pursue part of their degree courses at home and the latter part in the affiliated universities in Australia, the UK and the US. These affordable programmes came at an opportune time during the commodity crisis of the mid-1980s. World trade had deteriorated from the economic downturn in developed countries. Malaysia was badly affected as the prices of tin and palm oil, the country's main exports, plunged. The price of palm oil fell by 70% in 1986 from its high two years earlier.[3] The resulting recession led to a large number of corporate bankruptcies, loan defaults, and job losses.[4]

With the depreciation of the ringgit, these programmes were a welcome relief to cash-strapped parents. Studying in the local universities was not an option as there were limited places and the country's affirmative policy meant that the quota of placements for students from ethnic groups other than the majority Malays was limited. The twinning programme was the only route for many non-Malay middle-income families.

> I expected 500 students (when I started), but I only got 200.

As promising as it all was, Sunway College had a slow start. It took about 10 years before the institutions turned in a profit. "I expected 500 students (when I started), but I only got 200," Cheah recalled.

"I told my President, 'Wow! This is tough.' But we can't play around with people's children's education. So, we had to support it. We continued to make money from other sources to support the education side."

It was Cheah's deep belief in the value of education that kept him going. "I know education is not a closed-ended fund — after a certain time, you close it down. No, it cannot be. It is in perpetuity. I wanted

> I believe to have a fulfilling life you must have a higher purpose.

to build institutions of higher learning of repute that will still be here, continuing long after I'm gone."

In 1997, when the schools became self-sustaining, Cheah set up a trust, placing his shares in the entity. "At that time, foundations were not in vogue," he explained. But the intention never wavered, "I knew then that if I were to build a good institution of high repute it will be forever. And for that to happen, it meant that ownership had to be parked in perpetuity to a foundation."

He added, "I have no doubt that education is the best thing you can give an individual, to give them the opportunities to be better in life." This belief, coupled with his personal convictions, drove the Foundation to being. "I believe to have a fulfilling life you must have a higher purpose."

The Jeffrey Cheah Foundation was officially launched in 2010 with an endowment in perpetuity of all of the founder's equity in the education division of the Group, or about US$260 million. This makes it the biggest education-based social enterprise in the country.

To add greater credibility to the organisation, Cheah tapped on his network to rope in an illustrious group of academics, technocrats, and corporate figures as trustees. These included leading academic Professor Wang Gungwu of the National University of Singapore and Emeritus Professor of Australian National University; and economist and former deputy governor of the Central Bank of Malaysia, Dr Lin See-Yan. The Foundation also bears the royal seal of its patron, the Sultan of the state of Selangor, Sharafuddin Idris Shah.

As the schools began to do well, it attracted the attention, not just of students, local and international, but of bankers as well. Twenty years after the first school was set up, Cheah's bankers began urging him to list the business. After all, by that time, all of Sunway's business units had gone public, except for the construction company that was delisted in 2004 and floated again in 2015.

And being the owner of one of the largest private education organisations in the country, Cheah was told that an Initial Public Offering (IPO) would bankroll him further. "They would even say that the education group was the flavour of the year! 'List it and get a PE (price-earnings) of 20 or 25. You'll be worth RM1.5 to RM2 billion!'" Cheah recalled of the conversation with his bankers.

But he was not enticed. "This is not my intention. My intention is to put it in a foundation and it's for perpetuity. It's for society," he insisted.

Cheah had other practical reasons not to go public. "Now, if you list the company, the public shareholders will always want dividends. And when that happens, what will you do? All your men will have to compromise... on cost. So, you will not be able to deliver quality education."

Today, the Sunway Education Group runs 16 institutions, including two universities, one of which is Monash University's first campus outside of Australia; a school affiliated with renowned French culinary arts institution, Le Cordon Bleu; an international school and matriculation colleges. Revenues collected are in the range of US$175 million a year from 29,000 students, with enrolments growing at 10% a year.

For all the Group's successes, Cheah is as excited to talk about his Foundation as he is about his latest project in Iskandar. As a not-for-profit organisation, surpluses are channelled to the Foundation's work. "Not even one cent comes back to me," Cheah said. "In fact, I'm still ploughing money to put into Cambridge, Harvard, and Oxford to help the professorships so that I have good links with them."

> I want to put all that I have built in the education side into the Foundation in perpetuity so that it will one day be the Harvard of the East.

To date, seven professorships from these universities are endowed in perpetuity by the Foundation. In addition, there've been further collaborations with Harvard Medical School and the Sunway Medical Centre for training programmes for healthcare professionals in the region. With Cambridge University, Cheah has charted the institution's first foray to Asia with a research centre focused on Asian diseases. In addition, a scholarship has been set up in perpetuity with Oxford University aiding students from ASEAN studying Mathematical, Physical and Life Sciences.

Recently, the Foundation chalked up another milestone by contributing US$10 million to help establish a centre for sustainable development at Sunway University — the first of its kind in Asia. Holding court as chairman of the centre is Columbia University's Prof Jeffrey Sachs, one of the foremost proponents of sustainable development globally.

Needless to say, Cheah's ambitions for his Foundation are big. "I want to put all that I have built in the education side into the Foundation in perpetuity so that it will one day be the Harvard of the East," he said.

He's watching you

> I feel very satisfied seeing all these young men excel, given this opportunity.

It may come as a surprise to some that Cheah's interest in the Foundation extends beyond its set-up and vision right down to the minuscule details of individual students. The founder is known to sit in on selection interviews, particularly if the value of the scholarship is significant. The day before we met, he had personally interviewed a 19-year-old student who had been accepted into a top university in the UK for a four-year programme in engineering. Almost immediately after the interview, the decision was made.

"He is so well read!" Cheah enthused. "A 19-year-old talking like a businessman and an engineer!" The student was presented with an US$180,000 scholarship to Oxford University.

Every so often, he would also check on students' progress, like the one the Group sent to Cambridge in 2013 to read engineering on a scholarship worth US$160,000. "He is number two in Cambridge in the last exam. Fantastic!" Cheah beamed like a proud parent. "I feel very satisfied seeing all these young men excel, given this opportunity."

As of 2017, the Foundation says it has awarded US$85 million worth of scholarships to thousands of students to study in Sunway's institutions and some overseas.

Most of the scholarships are non-binding save for a handful of students each year who receive a significant quantum of financial aid. On their return, these high-calibre scholars work with the Group for at least five years.

For these special few, Cheah makes it a point to oversee their development in the company personally, for pragmatic reasons.

"If not, I'll lose them!" he said. "If I just park them with the manager, the manager may feel threatened by these intelligent young men."

Malaysia has been seeing an outflow of talent due to a variety of push and pull factors. For one, the attractive remuneration overseas together with the undervalued ringgit makes overseas employment compelling. Recruitment agency Hays says 93% of job seekers are willing to leave Malaysia for greener pastures for various reasons such as job opportunities, exposure, and lifestyle.[5]

Cheah's experience mirrors the news headlines. "To say I have no problems (attracting talent), I'd be lying. But, you know, I want the best. I want to work with the best. I want to learn from the best."

***

In the early years when Sunway Education first started, Cheah would walk into the chancellor's office checking on the number of students enrolled in his schools. Today, he is more interested in the number of scholarships given out.

I aspire to inspire before I expire.

For all the rich man's toys that he allows himself to indulge in — his supercars and his 77-foot yacht that sits on his still, 30-acre lake so he can enjoy nature without getting sea sick — Cheah remains grounded and clear about what he stands for. One of his favourite quotes that he rolls out on cue is, "I aspire to inspire before I expire."

You'd be hard pressed if you're hoping for Cheah to come up with a deep existential response to a life-changing event as the motivation for his giving. For him, it is as he says it is — education is the key to a brighter future for young lives and the satisfaction he gets seeing doors open for others spurs him on.

Instead of trying to understand his past to discover the "why" to his giving, it would be more insightful to look into his future to assess the "how," in particular, how he has set up the Foundation to last beyond him.

For that, you need look no further than his heir apparent, daughter Sarena. Not only has she been overseeing various aspects of the Group's businesses, Cheah had made it a point to involve her during the setup of the Foundation in the nitty gritty details of taxation, regulation, and funding. "If anything were to happen to me, she will be involved," he said. Cheah has ensured that his legacy is secured in perpetuity by law and it's execution by posterity.

So, it looks like his favourite quote needs a little tweaking to extend his tenure of inspiration — long *after* his expiration.

Notes

1 "Overview" 2015 Coutts Million Dollar Donor Report, <http://philanthropy.coutts.com/en/reports/2015/executive-summary.html>

2 "Asian Philanthropy and Wealth", 21 December 2015, Global Philanthropic, <https://asiapac.globalphilanthropic.com/blog/2015/12/asian-philanthropy-and-wealth/>

3 Kwame Sundaram Jomo, *Growth and Structural Change in the Malaysia Economy,* Palgrave Macmillan, 1990, p. 62.

4 Prema-chandra Athukorala, "Malaysia Economy in Three Crises", Working Papers in Trade and Development, Australia National University, October 2010.

5 In a purchasing parity survey conducted in 2015, ICT project managers in the UAE and the USA were earning 2.18 and 1.5 times, respectively, more than a person in a similar position in Malaysia. Closer to home in Thailand, Hong Kong and Singapore entry-level ICT project managers earned between 1.95 and 1.38 times more than the ones in Malaysia.

Chapter 22

Giving in All Seasons for All Reasons

Tahir

Tahir Foundation and Mayapada Group, Indonesia

It was the ancient philosopher, Aristotle, who said: "To give away money is an easy matter and in any man's power. But to decide to whom to give it and how large and when, and for what purpose and how, is neither in every man's power nor an easy matter."

Enter private banks and foundations to fill in the who-what-why-when-where-how of big giving.

But Indonesian billionaire, Tahir, who goes by only one name, makes light of the ancient's sagacity and the apparent administrative complexities of philanthropy. He facetiously disclaims any due process in his giving. "I do not know how to prioritise," he claims. "Just first in, first out."

Then a moment later, in all seriousness, he professed, "I have no right to choose."

Tahir has reportedly given away and pledged over US$200 million, a largesse that is as deep as it is wide.

Bounties and burdens

My meeting with Tahir took place in 2013 at his home in Singapore in the exclusive enclave of Sentosa. While the houses around his were palatial and ostentatious, his was relatively understated and unpretentious. For a second home outside of his home country of Indonesia, it would probably suffice. The interior of his home was furnished with modern simplicity, but what bore particular notice were the number of Boteros on the walls and around the home. While I admired the artworks, Tahir disclaimed any credit for it, attributing the good taste to his wife. The sophistication around the man stood out as much as the quiet affability he carries about him.

The son of makers of *becak*, the traditional three-wheeled rickshaw, Tahir was in his early 20s when he left for Singapore to pursue his tertiary education in Nantah, now known as Nanyang Technological University. His rise to Indonesia's rich list has been by fits and starts.

His first venture was a small one, trading goods between Indonesia and Singapore, while he was still in university. It was enough to fund his education in the island state. When he returned to Indonesia, he dabbled in the import business before becoming an agent for Suzuki automobiles. That business failed miserably and left him heavily in debt. It was the next venture in garment manufacturing that helped lift his fortunes as he took advantage of export quotas from the government.

At about the same time, Tahir was granted a banking license by the Indonesian government. In 1990, Bank Mayapada began operations and went public in 1997. Today, the bank is the 11th largest in the country with assets worth about US$4 billion. It has over 200 branches throughout the archipelago, with a market capitalisation of US$1.5 billion. In addition, the Group has expanded to two hospitals, in partnership with one of Singapore's most reputable hospital managers, and a chain of clinics to boot. Mayapada's portfolio also includes retail outlets with duty-free specialist DFS, a media arm that publishes *Forbes Indonesia*, as well as real estate. In 2016, Tahir bought two commercial properties at record prices in Singapore's central business district through his Singapore-listed property investment company, MYP. The price tag for the two buildings — US$420 million.

> I've a very strong inferiority complex.

Tahir also happens to be married to Rosy Riady, the eldest daughter of another of Indonesia's wealthiest, Mochtar Riady, founder of the Lippo Group (featured in Chapter 1). Tahir's association with the Riadys, particularly in the earlier years, dogged many of his achievements, with suspicions that it was through the Riadys that he built his business empire.

Reports have it that their marriage was arranged by Rosy's grandmother who approved of Tahir because his parents, like them, came from Fujian province in China. Her family thought well of his education and liked the prestige that came with his being an alumnus of Nantah.

Tahir has always denied receiving any loans, gifts or opportunities from his influential in-laws. In fact, a week after his wedding, Tahir was told preemptorily by his new father-in-law that he would have no share in the family business — a matter of Riady's business principle that excluded in-laws.[1]

"I've a very strong inferiority complex," Tahir deadpanned, when asked about his relationship with the Riadys.

"You know I'm a normal young guy married to a rich wife. In some instances, the wife may disrespect you because you depend too much on her family. Or your father-in-law or mother-in-law may not give you recognition because they think that you are too dependent on them. I do not want that. I want my wife to respect me and I want to gain [my parents-in-law's] recognition."

Having a close association with the Riadys has been both an asset and a liability for Tahir. While he admitted being known as the son-in-law of "Pak Mochtar" has ostensibly opened doors, it has also kept him on a tight rein. "If I didn't have rich or successful in-laws like the Riadys, I may live more peacefully. I may even live more joyfully; I can be more relaxed, you know. But I can't," he said, pointing out the irony of his predicament.

From large coffers to tiny hands

As much as critics would want to pour scorn on Tahir's business success, it's hard to cast aspersions on his giving, which has been a calling from young. "I came from a poor family," he revealed. "I had a strong will

212

and said 'If one day, by God's blessings, I can [be rich], I'd like to do something for my people.' Not only for my people, for everyone."

Tahir holds up his Christian faith as the motivation for his giving. He espouses himself as much to long-term preventive healthcare issues and education as he does to supporting individual families personally. He works through a foundation with a clear mandate but often gives beyond it.

The Tahir Foundation is dedicated to two specific causes — healthcare and education. Its most notable partnership is with the Bill and Melinda Gates Foundation, the American-based private charity with a US$40 billion endowment anchored by one of the world's richest couples. In 2013, the two parties agreed to set aside US$100 million each to fight AIDS, tuberculosis and malaria, and to tackle issues of reproduction, mainly in Indonesia.

Tahir declared the day he signed the Memorandum of Understanding with the Gates his "most joyful day."

"This was my dream," he said. "And the dream came true."

Through the Foundation, scholarships have also been presented through Tahir's alma mater, Nanyang Technological University, and grants encourage medical research between universities in Singapore and Indonesia.

Beyond education and healthcare, however, the Foundation says it supports a broad swath of projects including "those (that) advocate and execute our mission by presenting new ideas and long-term solutions for an improved Indonesia" — or code for any cause worth supporting at home.

The check list includes donations of double-decker tourist buses to the city of Jakarta, a fleet of vehicles for the disabled, as well as emergency funds for post-disaster relief of earthquake victims in Aceh.

Not a man to be limited by geography, in 2016, Tahir pledged US$10 million to the UN High Commissioner for Refugees (UNHCR) to provide education to refugee children around the world. He has visited the refugee camps in Jordan twice with donations of US$1 million. His contributions have made him the biggest Asian donor to the UNHCR.[2]

In the world of philanthropy, there are the givers who donate for the satisfaction they get from seeing lives changed before them. Then there are those who give to causes that are less popular because the

> If I send a student to the school and one day he graduates, I feel joy.

outcomes are less measurable. The benefits of contributions made to developmental initiatives like vaccinations, nutrition, access to contraceptives and gender equality are challenging to quantify. Trying to convert every dollar spent on vaccinations to economic benefits is just not the same as providing an education fund for a family and seeing the children in the graduation ceremony years later.

Bill and Melinda Gates, Tahir pointed out, are of those who give generously without immediate and apparent gratification. "Bill Gates doesn't get rewarded because his contribution is for prevention," he said. "He donates money to eradicate polio, but he doesn't know who gets healed, or in whom the disease was prevented."

By contrast, Tahir said, "If a needy person comes to see me, and I support him and he gets healed, I get rewarded. His healing gives me joy. If I send a student to the school and one day he graduates, I feel joy."

Comparing the extent of their magnanimity, Tahir conceded, self-effacingly, "I think (Gates) is greater than I. I'm nothing."

Never mind his donation to fight infectious diseases and address reproduction issues in Indonesia through the Gates' Foundation; and not to mention his US$14 million contribution to alleviate the Syrian refugee crisis, the outcomes of which would also be hard to account for.

But by admission, his greatest satisfaction is from the personal contact with his beneficiaries.

He recalled helping a pair of siblings whose parents were too poor to send them to school but were too proud to accept handouts. He had heard about them from people in the office as the family sold drinks by the road just outside one of his bank branches in Jakarta. To preserve their dignity, which he admired, Tahir presented the parents with a proposition — he would pay for the children's education. In return, the siblings would "work" in his branch for two hours every banking day. Work, it was later discovered, was being put in a room to complete their homework and revision. This went on for years and today, Tahir proudly announced, the two are a doctor and an engineer.

Not only does helping in this way gladden his heart, Tahir insists it's easy work. "This is a thing that you can do every day," he said. "You don't have to find time or a special opportunity to do good work. Monday is no better than Tuesday to do the work of philanthropy. You can do it 24 hours."

> You don't have to find time or a special opportunity to do good work.

True to self, in 2017, on another one of his trips to the Syrian refugee community in Jordan, he reconnected with a family he had met previously and offered a trust fund of US$200,00 to support the five children's tertiary education. It was to motivate the young ones to further their education — a goal the "adopted grandfather" had set for them.[3]

In a country that's been rated low in the area of institutional and regulatory infrastructure conducive to philanthropic efforts,[4] Tahir's largesse is an anomaly. While the practice of *zakat*, the Muslim obligation of giving to the poor dominates the charitable landscape in this the largest Islamic country in the world, little else seems to be moving in the direction of encouraging large, structured and systematic giving. And that is where Tahir's missionary zeal is directed as he has dedicated himself to spreading the message of giving among the wealthy.

"To be successful is not the goal. It is not the objective. It's only a process to reach another goal, which is to bless other people. That's the real objective of life," sums up Tahir.

And that's a message he preaches as much as he practices, as he finds more reasons, in any season, to bless.

Notes

1 "Dato' Sri Prof. Dr. Tahir: Being the son-in-law of Lippo Group founder", The Jakarta Post, 28 September 2015.

2 "Support from UNHCR Eminent Advocate Dato' Sri Tahir's to benefit refugees globally", UNHCR Public Information Unit, 18 May 2017, < http://www.unhcr.org/id/en/10500-support-from-unhcr-eminent-advocate-dato-sri-tahirs-to-benefit-refugees-globally.html>

3 Novan Iman Santosa, "More funds promised for Syrian refugees", The Jakarta Post, 4 April 2017.

4 *Doing Good Index 2018: Maximising Asia's Potential,* Centre for Asian Philanthropy & Society, p. 35.